WHY
DELIBERATIVE
DEMOCRACY?

WHY DELIBERATIVE DEMOCRACY?

AMY GUTMANN AND
DENNIS THOMPSON

PRINCETON UNIVERSITY PRESS

PRINCETON AND OXFORD

Copyright © 2004 by Princeton University Press
Published by Princeton University Press, 41 William Street,
Princeton, New Jersey 08540
In the United Kingdom: Princeton University Press,
3 Market Place, Woodstock, Oxfordshire OX20 1SY
All Rights Reserved

British Library Cataloging-in-Publication Data is available

This book has been composed in

Library of Congress Cataloging-in-Publication Data

Gutmann, Amy.
Why deliberative democracy? / Amy Gutmann and Dennis Thompson.
p.cm.
Includes bibliographical references and index.
ISBN 0-691-12018-8 (cloth: alk. paper)—ISBN 0-691-12019-6 (pbk.: alk. paper)
1. Democracy.   2. Representative government and representation.
3. Compromise (Ethics)   4. Political ethics.
5. Forums (Discussion and debate)   6. Democracy—United States.   I. Title.

JC423.G9255 2004
321.8—dc22   2004040048

Printed on acid-free paper. ∞

www.pup.princeton.edu

Printed in the United States of America

5   7   9   10   8   6

ISBN-13: 978-0-691-12019-5 (pbk.)

ISBN-10: 0-691-12019-6 (pbk.)

Contents

Preface

N o subject has been more discussed in political theory in the last two decades than deliberative democracy. We contributed to that discussion in the early years, and then, in 1996, coauthored a book, *Democracy and Disagreement*, published by Harvard University Press, in which we defended our conception of deliberative democracy. We were gratified by the extensive attention the book received from scholars in the field as well as from many general readers. In 1999, Oxford University Press published *Deliberative Politics*, edited by Stephen Macedo, a volume devoted entirely to discussions of *Democracy and Disagreement*. In that collection, which included the most penetrating critiques of our theory as well as further extensions of it, we responded to our critics and modified our theory in some respects. But the debate continued, and so did our writing. In subsequent articles, we dealt with additional criticisms, made further modifications, and, most important, sought to apply the conception to changing circumstances in public life.

The essays brought together here represent a selection of our contributions to the continuing discussion about the place of deliberative democracy in today's world. With the exception of chapter 2, all of these were written after the publication of *Democracy and Disagreement* and *Deliberative Politics*. The chapters appear, with only minor editorial changes, as they were originally published (see the Acknowledgments, on page 207). A complete list of our other jointly authored articles are listed on page 209, following the Acknowledgments.

"What Deliberative Democracy Means" (chapter 1) was written for this volume and has not previously been published. We intend it both as a general introduction for nontheorists who are interested in learning more about this conception of democracy, and as an overview for scholars who are seeking a relatively compact statement of the current state of the theory. We hope that it presents a balanced assessment, but we do not pretend that it is neutral in character. We do not hesitate to present our own views about the meaning of deliberative democracy.

"Moral Conflict and Political Consensus" (chapter 2) was one of the first contemporary works to analyze the practical and theoretical implications of the idea of democratic reciprocity, which forms the basis of many conceptions of deliberative democracy, including our own. Although we have used much of the argument of this essay later in the book in a modified form, we were encouraged to reprint the article because it has been widely cited in the literature and states an important view that stands on its own.

Chapters 3 and 4 are intended to advance the theoretical debate in different ways. "Deliberative Democracy beyond Process" (chapter 3) seeks to correct the common misunderstanding that deliberative democracy must be only procedural. We argue that any adequate conception must include not only procedural but also substantive principles, such as, in this case, liberty and opportunity. "Why Deliberative Democracy is Different" (chapter 4) emphasizes the dynamic character of deliberative democracy. Unlike most conceptions, it seeks to accommodate other theories, even those that may conflict with one another, because its basic principle of reciprocity makes room for ongoing moral conflict. Deliberative democracy is able to maintain its distinctive role as an adjudicator among conflicting theories because it treats its own principles as morally and politically provisional. (We have removed parts of the original sections on provisionality in this essay because we present our current views on this subject in chapters 1 and 3.) The last two chapters in this collection show how the theory of deliberative democracy can be applied to significant practical problems in contemporary public life—health care in the United States and in the United Kingdom, and transitional justice in South Africa.

In continuing to develop our theory of deliberative democracy, we have been most fortunate in the students and colleagues who have engaged with us over the years in print and in person. Some of those to whom we are indebted for advice on specific essays are listed at the beginning of the endnotes of those chapters. We are also grateful to the three reviewers of this book, to the commentators who contributed to *Deliberative Politics*, and to that volume's editor, Stephen Macedo. Sigal Ben-Porath oversaw the preparation of this manuscript for publication, and gave us valuable substantive comments on the first chapter, and helpful advice on which essays to include. We benefited greatly from the skill and judgment of the editors at Princeton University Press, especially Ian Malcolm. The book's production was expertly managed by Debbie Tegarden.

WHY
DELIBERATIVE
DEMOCRACY?

1

What Deliberative Democracy Means

To go to war is the most consequential decision a nation can make. Yet most nations, even most democracies, have ceded much of the power to make that decision to their chief executives— to their presidents and prime ministers. Legislators are rarely asked or permitted to issue declarations of war. The decision to go to war, it would seem, is unfriendly territory for pursuing the kind of reasoned argument that characterizes political deliberation.

Yet when President George W. Bush announced that the United States would soon take military action against Saddam Hussein, he and his advisors recognized the need to justify the decision not only to the American people but also to the world community. Beginning in October 2002, the administration found itself engaged in argument with the U.S. Congress and, later, with the United Nations. During the months of preparation for the war, Bush and his colleagues, in many different forums and at many different times, sought to make the case for a preventive war against Iraq.[1] Saddam Hussein, they said, was a threat to the United States because he had or could soon have weapons of mass destruction, and had supported terrorists who might have struck again against the United States. Further, he had tyrannized his own people and destabilized the Middle East.

In Congress and in the United Nations, critics responded, concurring with the judgment that Hussein was a terrible tyrant but challenging the administration on all its arguments in favor of going to war before exhausting the nonmilitary actions that might have controlled the threat. As the debate proceeded, it became clear that almost no one disagreed with the view that the world would be better off if Saddam Hussein no longer ruled in Iraq, but many doubted that he posed an imminent threat, and many questioned whether he actually supported the terrorists who had attacked or were likely to attack the United States.

This debate did not represent the kind of discussion that deliberative democrats hope for, and the deliberation was cut short once U.S. troops began their invasion in March 2003. Defenders and critics of the war seriously questioned one another's motives and deeply suspected that the reasons offered were really rationalizations for partisan politics. The administration, for its part, declined to wait until nonmilitary options had been exhausted, when a greater moral consensus might have been reached. But the remarkable fact is that even under the circumstances of war, and in the face of an alleged imminent threat, the government persisted in attempting to justify its decision, and opponents persevered in responding with reasoned critiques of a preventive war.

The critics are probably right that no amount of deliberation would have prevented the war, and the supporters are probably right that some critics would never have defended going to war even if other nonmilitary sanctions had ultimately failed. Yet the deliberation that did occur laid the foundation for a more sustained and more informative debate *after* the U.S. military victory than would otherwise have taken place. Because the administration had given reasons (such as the threat of the weapons of mass destruction) for taking action, critics had more basis to continue to dispute the original decision, and to challenge the administration's judgment. The imperfect deliberation that preceded the war prepared the ground for the less imperfect deliberation that followed.

Thus even in a less than friendly environment, deliberative democracy makes an appearance, and with some effect. Both the advocates and the foes of the war acted as if they recognized an obligation to justify their views to their fellow citizens. (That their motives were political or partisan is less important than that their actions were responsive to this obligation.) This problematic episode can help us discern the defining characteristics of deliberative democracy if we attend to both the presence and the absence of those characteristics in the debate about the war.

What Is Deliberative Democracy?

Most fundamentally, deliberative democracy affirms the need to justify decisions made by citizens and their representatives. Both are expected to justify the laws they would impose on one another. In a democracy, leaders should therefore give reasons for their decisions, and respond to the reasons that citizens give in return. But not all issues, all the time, require deliberation. Deliberative democracy makes room for many other forms of decision-making (including bargaining among groups, and secret operations ordered by executives), as long as the use of these forms themselves is justified at some point in a deliberative process. Its first and most important characteristic, then, is its *reason-giving* requirement.

The reasons that deliberative democracy asks citizens and their representatives to give should appeal to principles that individuals who are trying to find fair terms of cooperation cannot reasonably reject. The reasons are neither merely procedural ("because the majority favors the war") nor purely substantive ("because the war promotes the national interest or world peace"). They are reasons that should be accepted by free and equal persons seeking fair terms of cooperation.

The moral basis for this reason-giving process is common to many conceptions of democracy. Persons should be treated not merely as objects of legislation, as passive subjects to be ruled, but as autonomous agents who take part in the governance of their own society, directly or through their representatives. In deliberative democracy an important way these agents take part is by presenting and responding

3

to reasons, or by demanding that their representatives do so, with the aim of justifying the laws under which they must live together. The reasons are meant both to produce a justifiable decision and to express the value of mutual respect. It is not enough that citizens assert their power through interest-group bargaining, or by voting in elections. No one seriously suggested that the decision to go to war should be determined by logrolling, or that it should be subject to a referendum. Assertions of power and expressions of will, though obviously a key part of democratic politics, still need to be justified by reason. When a primary reason offered by the government for going to war turns out to be false, or worse still deceptive, then not only is the government's justification for the war called into question, so also is its respect for citizens.

A second characteristic of deliberative democracy is that the reasons given in this process should be *accessible* to all the citizens to whom they are addressed. To justify imposing their will on you, your fellow citizens must give reasons that are comprehensible to you. If you seek to impose your will on them, you owe them no less. This form of reciprocity means that the reasons must be public in two senses. First, the deliberation itself must take place in public, not merely in the privacy of one's mind. In this respect deliberative democracy stands in contrast to Rousseau's conception of democracy, in which individuals reflect on their own on what is right for the society as a whole, and then come to the assembly and vote in accordance with the general will.[2]

The other sense in which the reasons must be public concerns their content. A deliberative justification does not even get started if those to whom it is addressed cannot understand its essential content. It would not be acceptable, for example, to appeal only to the authority of revelation, whether divine or secular in nature. Most of the arguments for going to war against Iraq appealed to evidence and beliefs that almost anyone could assess. Although President Bush implied that he thought God was on his side, he did not rest his argument on any special instructions from his heavenly ally (who may or may not have joined the coalition of the willing).

Admittedly, some of the evidence on both sides of the debate was technical (for example, the reports of the U.N. inspectors).

But this is a common occurrence in modern government. Citizens often have to rely on experts. This does not mean that the reasons, or the bases of the reasons, are inaccessible. Citizens are justified in relying on experts if they describe the basis for their conclusions in ways that citizens can understand; and if the citizens have some independent basis for believing the experts to be trustworthy (such as a past record of reliable judgments, or a decision-making structure that contains checks and balances by experts who have reason to exercise critical scrutiny over one another).

To be sure, the Bush administration relied to some extent on secret intelligence to defend its decision. Citizens were not able at the time to assess the validity of this intelligence, and therefore its role in the administration's justification for the decision. In principle, using this kind of evidence does not necessarily violate the requirement of accessibility if good reasons can be given for the secrecy, and if opportunities for challenging the evidence later are provided. As it turned out in this case, the reasons were indeed challenged later, and found to be wanting. Deliberative democracy would of course have been better served if the reasons could have been challenged earlier.

The third characteristic of deliberative democracy is that its process aims at producing a decision that is *binding* for some period of time. In this respect the deliberative process is not like a talk show or an academic seminar. The participants do not argue for argument's sake; they do not argue even for truth's own sake (although the truthfulness of their arguments is a deliberative virtue because it is a necessary aim in justifying their decision). They intend their discussion to influence a decision the government will make, or a process that will affect how future decisions are made. At some point, the deliberation temporarily ceases, and the leaders make a decision. The president orders troops into battle, the legislature passes the law, or citizens vote for their representatives. Deliberation about the decision to go to war in Iraq went on for a long period of time, longer than most preparations for war. Some believed that it should have gone on longer (to give the U.N. inspectors time to complete their task). But at some point the president had to decide

5

whether to proceed or not. Once he decided, deliberation about the question of whether to go to war ceased.

Yet deliberation about a seemingly similar but significantly different question continued: was the original decision justified? Those who challenged the justification for the war of course did not think they could undo the original decision. They were trying to cast doubt on the competence or judgment of the current administration. They were also trying to influence future decisions—to press for involving the United Nations and other nations in the reconstruction effort, or simply to weaken Bush's prospects for reelection.

This continuation of debate illustrates the fourth characteristic of deliberative democracy—its process is *dynamic*. Although deliberation aims at a justifiable decision, it does not presuppose that the decision at hand will in fact be justified, let alone that a justification today will suffice for the indefinite future. It keeps open the possibility of a continuing dialogue, one in which citizens can criticize previous decisions and move ahead on the basis of that criticism. Although a decision must stand for some period of time, it is provisional in the sense that it must be open to challenge at some point in the future. This characteristic of deliberative democracy is neglected even by most of its proponents. (We discuss it further below in examining the concept of provisionality.)

Deliberative democrats care as much about what happens after a decision is made as about what happens before. Keeping the decision-making process open in this way—recognizing that its results are provisional—is important for two reasons. First, in politics as in much of practical life, decision-making processes and the human understanding upon which they depend are imperfect. We therefore cannot be sure that the decisions we make today will be correct tomorrow, and even the decisions that appear most sound at the time may appear less justifiable in light of later evidence. Even in the case of those that are irreversible, like the decision to attack Iraq, reappraisals can lead to different choices later than were planned initially. Second, in politics most decisions are not consensual. Those citizens and representatives who disagreed with the original decision are more likely to accept it if they believe they have a chance to reverse or modify it in the future. And they are more likely to be able to do so if they have a chance to keep making arguments.

One important implication of this dynamic feature of deliberative democracy is that the continuing debate it requires should observe what we call the principle of the economy of moral disagreement. In giving reasons for their decisions, citizens and their representatives should try to find justifications that minimize their differences with their opponents. Deliberative democrats do not expect deliberation always or even usually to yield agreement. How citizens deal with the disagreement that is endemic in political life should therefore be a central question in any democracy. Practicing the economy of moral disagreement promotes the value of mutual respect (which is at the core of deliberative democracy). By economizing on their disagreements, citizens and their representatives can continue to work together to find common ground, if not on the policies that produced the disagreement, then on related policies about which they stand a greater chance of finding agreement. Cooperation on the reconstruction of Iraq does not require that the parties at home and abroad agree about the correctness of the original decision to go to war. Questioning the patriotism of critics of the war, or opposing the defense expenditures that are necessary to support the troops, does not promote an economy of moral disagreement.

Combining these four characteristics, we can define deliberative democracy as a form of government in which free and equal citizens (and their representatives), justify decisions in a process in which they give one another reasons that are mutually acceptable and generally accessible, with the aim of reaching conclusions that are binding in the present on all citizens but open to challenge in the future.[3] This definition obviously leaves open a number of questions. We can further refine its meaning and defend its claims by considering to what extent deliberative democracy is democratic; what purposes it serves; why it is better than the alternatives; what kinds of deliberative democracy are justifiable; and how its critics can be answered.

7

How Democratic Is Deliberation?

In its origins, deliberative politics has an ambivalent relation to modern democracy. Its roots can be traced to fifth-century Athens. According to Pericles, political leaders then saw discussion not as a "stumbling-block in the way of action" but as an "indispensable preliminary to any wise action at all."[4] Aristotle was the first major theorist to defend the value of a process in which citizens publicly discuss and justify their laws to one another.[5] He argued that ordinary citizens debating and deciding together can reach a better decision than can experts acting alone. But the Athenian democracy of Pericles and Aristotle was quite different from ours. Only a small portion of the residents counted as citizens; many were slaves. The deliberation took place in an assembly open to all citizens, not in a legislature or in the campaigns that characterize democratic practice in our time. And though Aristotle saw the virtues of deliberation by the many, he preferred aristocracy, wherein the deliberators would be more competent, and the deliberation more refined.

In the early modern period, deliberation was more explicitly contrasted with democracy. When the term "deliberative" was first used to refer to political discussion (evidently as early as 1489), it referred to discussion within a small and exclusive group of political leaders. By the eighteenth century, deliberation was part of a defense of political representation that pointedly resisted appeals to popular opinion. Edmund Burke's "Speech to the electors of Bristol," which declared that "Parliament is a deliberative assembly," is famously a defense of a trustee conception of representation that today seems more aristocratic than democratic.[6] Neither did the founders of the new American nation embrace a fully democratic form of deliberation. The authors of the *Federalist Papers* certainly sought institutions that would promote deliberation. But although in the view of one commentator their constitutional design "combined deliberation and democracy,"[7] the degree of democracy they tolerated remained very much limited in scope and membership.

The most prominent nineteenth-century advocate of "government by discussion"—John Stuart Mill—is rightly considered one of the sources of deliberative democracy. But he too continued to prefer that this discussion be led by the better educated.[8] It was not until the early part of the twentieth century that deliberation came to be decisively joined to democracy. In the writings of John Dewey, Alf Ross, and A. D. Lindsay we finally find unequivocal declarations of the need for political discussion in a polity recognizably democratic in the modern sense. These theorists not only included widespread deliberation as part of democracy, but saw it as a necessary condition of this form of government. Lindsay regarded discussion as "the essential of democracy."[9]

More than any other theorist, Jürgen Habermas is responsible for reviving the idea of deliberation in our time, and giving it a more thoroughly democratic foundation. His deliberative politics is firmly grounded in the idea of popular sovereignty.[10] The fundamental source of legitimacy is the collective judgment of the people. This is to be found not in the expression of an unmediated popular will, but in a disciplined set of practices defined by the deliberative ideal. Some critics, however, complain that his conception does not adequately protect liberal values, such as freedom of religion or human rights. His proceduralism, the critics suggest, realizes democracy at the expense of liberalism. They believe that a theory of justice like that of John Rawls provides a more secure foundation for these values without denying the legitimate claims of democracy.

We note later that Habermas and Rawls are not so far apart as this contrast suggests. But here the point to keep in mind is that the democratic element in deliberative democracy should turn not on how purely procedural the conception is but on how fully inclusive the process is. While deliberation is now happily married to democracy— and Habermas deserves much of the credit for making the match—the bond that holds the partners together is not pure proceduralism. What makes deliberative democracy democratic is an expansive definition of who is included in the process of deliberation—an inclusive answer to the questions of who has the right (and effective opportunity) to deliberate or choose the deliberators, and to whom do the deliberators owe their justifications. In this respect, the traditional tests of democratic inclusion, applied to deliberation itself, constitute the primary criterion of the extent to which deliberation is democratic. (It must be said, however, that this defense of deliberative democracy does not suffice to show that it has overcome its aristocratic origins. One of the recurring objections, which we take up later, is that deliberative democracy is exclusive in various ways, excluding some people not by legal or formal restrictions as early deliberative politics did, but by informal norms defining what counts as proper deliberation.)

What Purposes Does Deliberative Democracy Serve?

The general aim of deliberative democracy is to provide the most justifiable conception for dealing with moral disagreement in politics. In pursuing this aim, deliberative democracy serves four related purposes. The first is to promote the legitimacy of collective decisions. This aim is a response to one of the sources of moral disagreement—scarcity of resources. Citizens would not have to argue about how best to distribute health care or who should receive organ transplants if these goods and services were unlimited. In the face of scarcity, deliberation can help those who do not get what they want, or even what they need, to come to accept the legitimacy of a collective decision.

The hard choices that public officials have to make should be more acceptable, even to those who receive less than they deserve, if everyone's claims have been considered on the merits, rather than on the basis of the party's bargaining power. Even with regard to decisions with which many disagree, most of us take one attitude toward those that are adopted after careful consideration of the relevant conflicting moral claims, and quite a different attitude toward those that are adopted merely by virtue of the relative strength of competing political interests.

The second purpose of deliberation is to encourage public-spirited perspectives on public issues. This aim responds to another source of moral disagreement—limited generosity. Few people are

10

inclined to be wholly altruistic when they are arguing about contentious issues of public policy, such as defense spending or health-care priorities. Deliberation in well-constituted forums responds to this limited generosity by encouraging participants to take a broader perspective on questions of common interest.

To be sure, politicians are not automatically transformed from representatives of special interests into trustees of the public interest as a result of talking to one another. The background conditions in which the deliberation takes place are critical. Deliberation is more likely to succeed to the extent that the deliberators are well informed, have relatively equal resources, and take seriously their opponents' views. But even when the background conditions are unfavorable (as they often are), citizens are more likely to take a broader view of issues in a process in which moral reasons are traded than in a process in which political power is the only currency.

The third purpose of deliberation is to promote mutually respectful processes of decision-making. It responds to an often neglected source of moral disagreement—incompatible moral values. Even fully altruistic individuals trying to decide on the morally best standards for governing a society of abundance would not be able to reconcile some moral conflicts beyond a reasonable doubt. They would still confront, for example, the problem of abortion, which pits the value of life against the value of liberty. Even issues of national security can pose questions about which people can reasonably disagree—under what conditions is a nation justified in starting a war, on its own, against another nation?

Deliberation cannot make incompatible values compatible, but it can help participants recognize the moral merit in their opponents' claims when those claims have merit. It can also help deliberators distinguish those disagreements that arise from genuinely incompatible values from those that can be more resolvable than they first appear. And it can support other practices of mutual respect, such as the economy of moral disagreement described earlier.

Inevitably, citizens and officials make some mistakes when they take collective actions. The fourth purpose of deliberation is to

11

help correct these mistakes. This aim is a response to the fourth source of disagreement, incomplete understanding. A well-constituted deliberative forum provides an opportunity for advancing both individual and collective understanding. Through the give-and-take of argument, participants can learn from each other, come to recognize their individual and collective misapprehensions, and develop new views and policies that can more successfully withstand critical scrutiny. When citizens bargain and negotiate, they may learn how better to get what they want. But when they deliberate, they can expand their knowledge, including both their self-understanding and their collective understanding of what will best serve their fellow citizens.

It is all too easy to assume that we already know what constitutes the best resolution of a moral conflict, and do not need to deliberate with our fellow citizens. To presume that we know what the right resolution is before we hear from others who will also be affected by our decisions is not only arrogant but also unjustified in light of the complexity of the issues and interests that are so often at stake. If we refuse to give deliberation a chance, not only do we forsake the possibility of arriving at a genuine moral compromise but we also give up the most defensible ground we could have for maintaining an uncompromising position: that we have fairly tested our views against those of others.

Tugging on the coattails of Thomas Jefferson, a little boy (in a *New Yorker* cartoon) once asked: "If you take those truths to be self-evident, then why do you keep on harping on them so much?" The answer from a deliberative perspective is that such claims deserve their status as self-evident truths for the purposes of collective action only if they can withstand challenge in a public forum. Jefferson himself argued for open deliberative forums, indeed even periodic constitutional conventions, in which citizens could contest conventional wisdom.[11] An implication of taking the problem of incomplete understanding seriously is that the results of the deliberative process should be regarded as provisional. Some results are rightly regarded as more settled than others. We do not have to reargue the question of slavery every generation. But the justification for regarding such results as settled is that they have met the deliberative challenge in the past, and there is no reason to believe that they could not do so today.

Why Is Deliberative Democracy Better Than Aggregative Democracy?

To appreciate the value of deliberative democracy, we need to consider the alternatives. Obviously, there are many conceptions of democracy, and many moral theories that support these conceptions. To begin, we should distinguish first- and second-order theories.[12] First-order theories seek to resolve moral disagreement by demonstrating that alternative theories and principles should be rejected. The aim of each is to be the lone theory capable of resolving moral disagreement. The most familiar theories of justice—utilitarianism, libertarianism, liberal egalitarianism, communitarianism—are first-order theories in this sense. Each theory claims to resolve moral conflict, but does so in ways that require rejecting the principles of its rivals. In contrast, deliberative democracy is best understood as a second-order theory. Second-order theories are *about* other theories in the sense that they provide ways of dealing with the claims of conflicting first-order theories. They make room for continuing moral conflict that first-order theories purport to eliminate. They can be held consistently without rejecting a wide range of moral principles expressed by first-order theories. Deliberative democracy's leading rivals among second-order theories are what are known as aggregative conceptions of democracy.[13]

The deliberative conception, as we have indicated, considers the reasons that citizens and their representatives give for their expressed preferences. It asks for justifications. The aggregative conception, by contrast, takes the preferences as given (though some versions would correct preferences based on misinformation). It requires no justification for the preferences themselves, but seeks only to combine them in various ways that are efficient and fair. Some preferences may be discounted or even rejected, but only because they do

13

not produce an optimal result, not because they are not justified by reasons.

The best way to reveal the essential differences between these conceptions is to examine their responses to the basic problem of democratic politics that both of them purport to address—how to make legitimate decisions for the society as a whole in the face of fundamental disagreement. The core of the problem is not merely that people disagree, but that some of the disagreement is reasonable.[14] It is built into the circumstances of social and political life. When citizens disagree about such issues as the morality of abortion, capital punishment, starting a preventive war, or funding health care, deliberation does not produce agreement, and perhaps even should not.[15] Let us assume, then, that there are some disagreements that at any particular time cannot be resolved by deliberation. Yet governments must make decisions. How should they decide?

Aggregative theories offer two seemingly different but closely related methods. The first is a form of majoritarianism: put the question to the people and let them vote (or let them record their preferences in public opinion surveys).[16] The most common version of this method is to let the representatives of the people make the decision, again by majority vote, or some similar rule, in the legislature. The representatives themselves are chosen in elections, which are viewed as "competitive struggle[s] for the people's vote."[17] The electoral process is modeled on the analogy of the market. Like producers, politicians and parties formulate their positions and devise their strategies in response to the demands of voters who, like consumers, express their preferences by choosing among competing products (the candidates and their parties). Whatever debate takes place in the campaign serves a function more like that of advertising (informing the voters about the comparative advantages of the candidates) than like that of argument (seeking to change minds by giving reasons).

The second aggregative method gives less deference to the votes and opinions of citizens: officials take note of the expressed preferences but put them through an analytic filter—such as cost-benefit analysis—which is intended to produce optimal outcomes. In some versions of this process, preferences based on misinformation or faulty heuristics can be corrected, and sets of preferences that produce irrational results (such as cyclical majorities) can be modified. This method originates in classical utilitarianism and owes its contemporary pedigree to welfare economics. But it is not necessarily democratic. Giving voters the final word is not the most rational way to produce policies and laws that maximize welfare. Experts may be more competent at finding laws and policies that serve that end. But proponents of this method usually welcome democratic procedures such as elections, because they recognize that experts and the politicians who appoint them cannot always be trusted to pursue the public interest.

What these methods have in common—and what defines aggregative conceptions—is that they take the expressed preferences as the privileged or primary material for democratic decision-making. Preferences as such do not need to be justified, and aggregative conceptions pay little or no attention to the reasons that citizens or their representatives give or fail to give. They regard reasons as significant only insofar as the reasons help predict or correct preferences. (The reasons might, for example, enable politicians to anticipate future preferences, or they might help analysts identify preferences that are based on misinformation.) Aggregative theorists thus believe that the collective outcomes produced by their various methods need no further justification beyond the rationale for the method itself. The majoritarian or utilitarian assumptions underlying the method provide its justification. Reasons can be given for the outcomes, but they are to be found not in the preferences but in the rationale for the method of combining the preferences.

Aggregative conceptions have important advantages. First, they produce determinate outcomes, at least in principle.[18] The result of an election or the conclusion of a cost-benefit analysis yields definite decisions. This is no small advantage in dealing with the problem of disagreement, especially in disputes that are not resolvable on reasonable terms. Deliberative democrats recognize of course that decisions must be made—even when the reason-giving

15

process is incomplete. On any conception of democracy, elections must be held, and in elections citizens express their will without giving reasons. But deliberative democrats tend to emphasize the provisionality of political outcomes more than their finality.

A second advantage of aggregative conceptions is that they rely on relatively uncontroversial procedures to resolve disagreement. They also provide ways of reaching decisions that can be said to express the views of most citizens, and may even be regarded as fair under the circumstances. The methods of aggregative democrats are not morally neutral, as they sometimes claim, but the methods do not entail positions on most substantive issues, and do not pass moral judgment on the individual preferences that citizens express, however base or noble they may be. The most common methods take preferences as given, and therefore can be said to be less paternalistic. Even the methods that correct the preferences still seek to respect what citizens or voters actually desire, or would desire if they were better informed—not what they should desire if they were more public spirited or if they were more inclined to respect the principle of reciprocity.

Despite these substantial advantages, the aggregative conception is seriously flawed, and cannot serve as a principled basis for democratic decision-making. By taking existing or minimally corrected preferences as given, as the base line for collective decisions, the aggregative conception fundamentally accepts and may even reinforce existing distributions of power in society. These distributions may or may not be fair, but aggregative conceptions do not offer any principles by which we can decide. Even more important, they do not provide any process by which citizens' views about those distributions might be changed.

A second fundamental problem of aggregative conceptions is that they do not provide any way for citizens to challenge the methods of aggregation themselves. The "preference" for a different method of decision-making—the argument for a deliberative process, for example—cannot be treated in the same fashion as other preferences are, and simply factored into a cost-benefit analysis.[19] The argument rejects in critical respects the assumptions of such an analysis. Furthermore, aggregative methods do not welcome all kinds of primary preferences equally. Those that can be readily translated into economic categories fit much better than those that express values that are incommensurable. Sometimes governments have to put a price on life and health, but they have to recognize that the value of life and health is not completely captured by their price, even in decision-making about public policy. Even on their own terms, then, aggregative methods do not always answer the critical question decision-makers must ask: should a government give priority, for example, to treating conditions that are not life-threatening but cause large numbers of people considerable discomfort, or to treating conditions that are life-threatening but affect only small numbers of people?

Consider the problem the state of Oregon faced in the early 1990s: how to allocate the state's limited resources for health care for residents enrolled in Medicaid. To set priorities for its publicly funded health care under Medicaid, the Oregon Health Services Commission created a list of several hundred conditions and treatments, ranked mainly on the basis of cost-benefit calculations. Treatments lower on the list were regarded as less cost-beneficial than those higher on the list, and therefore less likely to receive funding. In essence, the Commission followed the second kind of method recommended by aggregative democrats. The ranking did not correspond to popular opinion about what the most serious diseases are: some life-threatening conditions ranked lower because their treatment was relatively expensive or affected relatively small numbers of people. But the ranking was a good-faith attempt to maximize the welfare of the largest number of citizens, given the limited resources the state had at its disposal.

The list of priorities provoked a public outcry. Health policy that followed these priorities might maximize the welfare of most citizens, but the rankings departed so far from what most citizens thought was right or fair that no state official could continue to justify the policy. Capping a tooth ranked much higher than an appendectomy, for example. The Commission might have reverted to the first method recommended by aggregative democrats—conducting a

17

survey or referendum and taking the results as final. But the Commission realized that public opinion on this complex set of issues was inchoate, and would depend on how the questions were phrased. Instead, the Commission wisely enlisted the aid of the methods of deliberative democracy.

The Commission undertook an elaborate process of consultation. It sponsored community meetings at which participants were "asked to think and express themselves in the first person plural . . . as members of a statewide community for whom health care has a shared value." Deliberation went through stages, as leaders presented their proposals, citizens responded, leaders revised, citizens reacted. This is what we call the reiteration of deliberation. It is an illustration of the dynamic character of deliberation. Eventually, the Commission presented a revised list, one that most observers deemed an improvement over the original plan.

Yet the Oregon experience should remind us that deliberative democracy is not a perfect way to deal with the problem of moral disagreement. (We defer until a later section discussion of the general criticisms of deliberative democracy, and consider here only two objections that are most relevant to the comparison with aggregative conceptions.) First, deliberative democracy does not provide a natural way to come to a definite conclusion short of consensus, which is not to be expected in most cases of decision-making. Deliberative politics almost always has to be supplemented by other decision procedures—in the Oregon case by a recommendation of a commission and a vote by the legislature. The community groups provided helpful input, which informed the further deliberations by both the Commission and the legislature, but in the end the disagreement that remained had to be resolved by a majority vote in the legislature. Deliberation must end in a decision, but deliberative democracy does not itself specify a single procedure for reaching a final decision. It must rely on other procedures, most notably voting, which in themselves are not deliberative.

Second, the deliberative conception relies on explicitly moral principles rather than the seemingly neutral ones of aggregative conceptions. Reciprocity is an explicitly moral principle. Deliberation therefore invokes substantive moral claims that may be independent of the preferences citizens put forward. In the Oregon episode, the most serious flaw in the proposed policy was not the ranking of treatments per se, but the unfairness of rationing under these circumstances. Because only citizens below certain income levels were eligible for any support at all, the rationing necessary at the relatively low level of funding available would cause some poor citizens to lose out to other poor citizens. Some of the participants in the deliberative process recognized that this was unfair, but to express that recognition they had to appeal at least implicitly to a principle of justice that not everyone accepted. Furthermore, in order to eliminate this unfairness they had to call for an increase in the total budget for health care—an option that went beyond the agreed-upon agenda of the community meetings.

Neither of these disadvantages is fatal to the case for deliberative democracy, however. Indeed, the problems each identifies can be turned to the advantage of deliberative democracy. The fact that deliberative democracy does not in itself define a unique method for bringing deliberation to a justified conclusion (short of a moral consensus) means that it acknowledges that no single method can justify whatever results from its implementation. No decision-making method, for example, should be able to justify a war of aggression. Deliberative democracy can accommodate many different kinds of decision-making procedures to reach final decisions, including voting and executive order, provided they are justified in a deliberative forum. More important, the open-ended nature of deliberation enables citizens or legislators to challenge earlier decisions, including decisions about the procedures for making decisions. Deliberative democracy's provisionality checks the excesses of conventional democracy's finality.

The appeal to justice and other potentially controversial principles may intensify the disagreement that exists, but it can also lead to new ways of dealing with it, ways that would otherwise have been neglected. In the Oregon case, the deliberative process forced officials and citizens to confront a serious problem of injustice that they had previously evaded—the unfairness of a harsh rationing scheme that affected only poor citizens. As a result, the basic unfairness in the policy

19

was somewhat lessened in a way that neither most of the critics of the plan nor its proponents expected. When the legislators finally saw what treatments on the list would have to be curtailed or eliminated under the projected budget, they managed to find more resources, and increased the total budget for health care for the poor. Apart from the results, the year-long deliberations helped citizens, legislators, and health-care professionals come to a better understanding of their own values—those they shared and those they did not. They were able, as they went forward, to confront the difficult decisions they had to make about health-care policy, to work together in a more cooperative "first person plural" spirit. The continuing process also exposed another glaring defect of the original process—the absence of the poor citizens who would be most affected by the policy. It became clearer that in the future they should be more adequately represented in the process.

In the face of disagreement, deliberative democracy tells citizens and their representatives to continue to reason together. If the disagreement is resolvable on reciprocal terms, deliberation is more likely than aggregation to produce agreement. If it is not so resolvable, deliberation is more likely than aggregation to produce justifiable agreement in the future, and to promote mutual respect when no agreement is possible. By engaging in deliberation, citizens acknowledge the possibility that they may change their preferences. The preferences that they assert now may not be the preferences they find they wish to express later. The very nature of the deliberative process of justification sends a signal that its participants are willing to enter into a dialogue in which the reasons given, and the reasons responded to, have the capacity to change minds.

On many disagreements, especially reasonable ones, people will not change their minds, no matter how respectfully they deliberate with their opponents. If citizens persist in defending the position with which they began, what difference does it make if they come to regard their opponents' positions as morally reasonable? This thicker kind of respect encourages citizens to consider their opponents' positions on the merits, rather than to try to explain them as products of unfavorable conditions, such as impaired judgment, misguided motives, or cultural influences. Such an attitude is more conducive to appreciating that even benevolent and intelligent but fallible people are likely to disagree on morally difficult matters such as military intervention and heath-care policy—as well as abortion, capital punishment, affirmative action, and many other overtly moral issues. Moreover, considering positions on their merits generally builds a stronger basis for respect for persons than explaining positions as a product of unfavorable conditions. Certainly, some disagreements are the result of such conditions, and when a position can be shown to be justifiable mainly from a perspective that depends on such conditions, mutual respect (of both persons and positions) does not prevent, and may require, that the critics of the position point out its defective origins. But in the absence of a specific showing of this kind, the presumption of respectful deliberation is that positions should be challenged on their merits.

What Kind of Deliberative Democracy?

Deliberative democrats have to deal with another kind of disagreement—not among citizens but among themselves. They disagree about the value, status, aims, and scope of deliberation, and their disagreements yield different versions of the theory of deliberative democracy. Some of these differences, we suggest, can be reconciled, and some cannot. In either case, recognizing the differences can help clarify the nature of both the theory and the practice of deliberative democracy.

Instrumental or Expressive?

Deliberative democrats disagree about whether deliberation has only instrumental value, as a means of arriving at good policies, or whether it also has expressive value, as a manifestation of mutual respect among citizens. On the instrumental view (sometimes called the epistemic view), deliberating about political issues has no value in itself. It is valuable only to the extent that it enables citizens to make the most justifiable political decisions.[20] On the expressive

21

view of deliberation, significant value resides in the act of justifying laws and public policies to the people who are bound by them.[21] By deliberating with one another, decision-makers manifest mutual respect toward their fellow citizens.

When the Oregon Commission consulted with community members about alternative proposals for funding health-care services, citizens could reasonably expect that Commission members would arrive at better outcomes than when they decided, without public deliberation, to rank capping teeth above treating acute appendicitis. The same citizens could also reasonably believe that the Commission's deliberation promoted a value basic to any democratic government—the expression of mutual respect between decision-makers and their fellow citizens. By their willingness to exchange views before rendering a binding decision, the commission members treated their fellow Oregonians as subjects, not merely objects, of decision-making. Had the Commission acted without deliberation, the value of this expression of mutual respect would have been lost, however correct or just the policy might have been.

These two views of the values that deliberative democracy is supposed to promote are not incompatible. Indeed, any adequate theory must recognize both. If deliberation tended to produce worse decisions than other processes in the long run, then it would not serve the expressive purpose. A process that generally produced bad outcomes would hardly express mutual respect. Citizens might participate on equal terms, but with results that few would see as worthy. The value would at best be like the faint satisfaction that players feel on a team that constantly loses its games. The instrumental view reminds us that because the stakes of political decision-making are high, and deliberation is a time-consuming activity, a deliberative process should contribute to fulfilling the central political function of making good decisions and laws.

But if we were to regard deliberation as only instrumental, we would fail to recognize the moral significance of the political fact that the decisions of government bind people other than the decision-makers themselves. Political officials cannot rightly decide an issue simply by claiming that they know that their preferred policies are right for their fellow citizens. They need to seek the views of those citizens who have to live with the results of the policies. When binding decisions are routinely made without deliberation, the government not only conveys disrespect for citizens, but also exposes its lack of adequate justification for imposing the decision on them. Furthermore, there is a practical reason for officials to recognize the expressive value of deliberation: they can thereby increase the likelihood not only of discovering but also of implementing good public policy. If citizens perceive that their views are not being respected, they may seek to block otherwise good policies.

If political deliberation tends to produce better decisions in the long run, and if political decision-makers in a democracy owe justifications to those who are bound by their decisions, then the instrumental and expressive rationales for deliberation can be mutually supportive. By deliberating with their fellow citizens, decision-makers can arrive at better, more adequately justified decisions and, in the process, express mutual respect among free and equal citizens.

The instrumental and expressive values cannot of course be reconciled in practice in every particular case. A deliberative process that otherwise expresses mutual respect can nonetheless produce an unjust outcome. And a nondeliberative process can produce a more nearly just result in some cases. Yet deliberative democracy, as we shall see, has the capacity both to criticize unjust outcomes and to recognize its own limits. In this way it tends, over time, to reconcile its own instrumental and expressive values.

Procedural or Substantive?

Another, closely related conflict that has divided deliberative democrats can also be resolved more readily than has usually been assumed. This conflict concerns the status of the principles of the theory: should they be procedural or substantive? Pure proceduralism holds that the principles should apply only to the process of making political decisions in government or civil society.[22] Thus the principles should not prescribe the substance of the laws, but only the procedures by which laws (such as equal suffrage) are made and

23

the conditions necessary for the procedures to work fairly (such as free political speech). Democratic theory, the proceduralists hold, should not incorporate substantive principles such as individual liberty or equal opportunity because such constraints are not necessary to ensure a fair democratic process. Pure proceduralists do not deny that substantive principles such as freedom of religion, nondiscrimination, or basic health care are important, but they insist on keeping these principles out of their democratic theory.

Deliberative theorists who favor a more substantive conception deny that procedural principles are sufficient. They point out that procedures (such as majority rule) can produce unjust outcomes (such as discrimination against minorities). Unjust outcomes, they assume, should not be justifiable on any adequate democratic theory. A theory that allows for the possibility that such outcomes are justified should be especially objectionable to deliberative democrats. A fundamental aim of deliberative democracy is to offer reasons that can be accepted by free and equal persons seeking fair terms of cooperation. Such reasons could rarely justify unjust outcomes. The idea of free and equal personhood itself provides substantive moral content for principles that would reject an unjust decision even if it had been reached by procedurally just means.

The reasons most often offered in defense of both substantive and procedural principles are associated with liberalism, broadly speaking. They reflect what it means to respect individuals as free and equal citizens. Those rights that are fundamental to human agency, dignity, or integrity (freedom of religion, racial nondiscrimination, and so on) need to be secured, along with rights related to the procedural aspects of democracy (such as the right to vote). Appreciating that majoritarian procedures can support aggressive wars, racial or religious discrimination, and other patently unjust policies, the principles of deliberative democracy, the substantive theorists insist, must go beyond process.[23]

A purely procedural conception of deliberative democracy, on its face, shares with aggregative theories the advantage of minimalism. Once the right procedures are in place, whatever emerges from them is right. It follows that if majority rule is right, then so are its results. But few pure proceduralists defend pure majority rule. Much like aggregative theorists, pure proceduralists usually support a more complex procedural conception, and they also offer reasons other than minimalism in its defense. To oppose the inclusion of substantive principles, they invoke a particular view of moral and political authority. Who has the authority to legislate in a democracy? Democratic citizens, not democratic theorists, pure proceduralists answer. Citizens or their representatives, within broad procedural limits, should be as free as possible to determine the content of laws. The substantive principles that some theorists would include in their conceptions of deliberative democracy in effect preempt the moral and political authority of citizens. Racial and religious discrimination and aggressive wars are usually wrong, but the questions of whether a particular law or decision should be so described, or whether the wrong decision should be overridden by more compelling considerations, should be left to citizens and their accountable representatives, not to theorists and their substantive principles. A deliberative theory that includes substantive principles, so the argument goes, improperly constrains democratic decision-making, including the process of deliberation itself.

Substantive theorists reply that the principles they propose are no less fundamental and no more contestable than the principles on which proceduralists rely. Procedural principles have substantive content, too. If majority rule is better than minority rule, it must be for moral reasons. These reasons refer to such values as free and equal personhood, the same values that support substantive principles. How procedural principles should be interpreted and how they should be applied are often controversial, and reasonably so. Procedural theories therefore cannot occupy a privileged place relative to substantive theories. Procedural and substantive principles alike require democratic deliberation, at least with respect to how they should be interpreted and applied. Both threaten to usurp legitimate democratic authority if they are put forward, without benefit of democratic deliberation, as morally and politically authoritative.

It follows that if the moral and political authority of free and equal citizens is to be safeguarded, then neither procedural nor substantive principles of deliberative democracy can claim priority. Both need to be treated as morally and politically provisional (in ways that we explain more fully below). Procedural and substantive principles should both be systematically open to revision in an on-going process of moral and political deliberation. If the principles are understood in this way, the usual objections against including substantive principles lose their force. The provisional status of all principles, procedural and substantive alike, thus constitutes a distinctive strength of deliberative theory, and at the same time offers deliberative democrats an effective way of uniting procedural and substantive principles into a coherent theory.

The contrast between procedural and substantive theories of democracy is sometimes thought to be reflected in a disagreement between Jürgen Habermas and John Rawls. Habermas is said to favor democratic deliberation over individual rights, and Rawls, rights over deliberation. But on the more careful interpretations of their theories, neither Habermas nor Rawls defends a purely procedural or purely substantive conception of democracy. As Habermas writes: ". . . private and public autonomy mutually presuppose each other in such a way that neither human rights nor popular sovereignty can claim primacy over its counterparts."[24] The democracy that Rawls defends is also fundamentally committed to securing both substantive and procedural principles.[25] The convergence between Habermas and Rawls suggests that the most compelling theories of deliberative democracy combine both substantive and procedural principles. They also both recognize that all democratic principles require substantive defense.

Consensual or Pluralist?

The disagreement among deliberative democrats who seek consensus and those who accept pluralism is more intractable than the disputes we have so far considered. Should deliberation aim at achieving consensus through realizing a common good or through seeking the fairest terms of living with a recalcitrant pluralism?

Deliberative democrats who identify with the republican tradition or with communitarianism in political theory typically seek a comprehensive or thick common good, one that goes beyond agreement on basic principles, whether procedural or substantive.[26] They do not assume that we will reach this goal, but they believe that it is nevertheless a worthy aim. It fulfills the deepest moral promise of deliberative democracy—a form of cooperation that all citizens could accept despite their deep differences of identity. Other deliberative democrats, drawing on the liberal tradition, argue that it is not always desirable to seek a comprehensive common good rather than to try to live respectfully with moral disagreements. One reason, they point out, is that some of these disagreements are inherent in the human condition. They arise because of our incomplete and incompatible moral and empirical understandings.[27]

Virtually all deliberative democrats can agree that a primary aim of deliberation is to justify decisions and laws that citizens and their representatives impose on one another. In this sense, deliberative democrats share a consensus that deliberation aims at least at a thin conception of the common good. Finding fair terms of cooperation among free and equal persons is a common good for both individuals and society as a whole.

This agreement among deliberative democrats breaks down when we ask whether the common good can or should be comprehensive. Consensus democrats recognize that a comprehensive common good is an ideal and will not often, if ever, be achieved, but they regard the failure to achieve it as a sign of defects that can and should be remedied, whether they lie in the capacities of citizens and their representatives or in the practices and institutions of the polity. Consensus democrats also tend to resist the idea, which pluralists willingly embrace, that a great deal of political disagreement is built into the conditions of collective life, and that to eliminate it entirely would be undesirable. Consensus democrats criticize pluralists for settling for too thin a conception of the common good. Agreement on fair terms of cooperation, they argue, does not create a community in which citizens find common ground at the deepest level of their social identities. It does not even require citizens to engage deeply with one another over their deepest moral differences. They must set these differences aside, the pluralists are assumed to say, in

27

order to find fair terms of cooperation and to arrive at just decisions and laws. The pluralists' common good therefore does not serve even deliberation itself well. A thin pluralist conception of the common good produces passive citizens, the consensus democrats argue, who too readily settle for the role of consumers of material commodities, rather than producers of public goods.

Pluralists reply that a democracy that seeks a comprehensive good threatens to become tyrannical. If moral differences are as deep and pervasive as pluralists believe, they can be eliminated in politics only by repression. As long as people in power and those to whom they are accountable are neither omniscient nor angelic, and as long as they reasonably disagree about how to rank incompatible values, deliberation should aim at achieving a noncomprehensive common good, and at finding good ways of living with ongoing moral disagreements. If deliberators aimed primarily at a comprehensive common good, they would be tempted to tolerate less diversity than the disharmonious moral universe demands.

Although pluralists agree that deliberation should strive to justify as much agreement as possible, they also seek ways of living well with those disagreements that cannot or should not be eliminated at any given time. This is the deep and irreconcilable difference between democrats who accept pluralism as part of the human condition and those who see it always as a serious political problem to be overcome by deliberation. Some disagreements—for example, a call to exclude blacks, Jews, or homosexuals from various associations—cry out for a democracy to confirm its commitment to the principles of nondiscrimination and equal opportunity in their core form. But other disagreements should not be resolved. We call these deliberative disagreements: they involve conflicts not between views that are clearly right and clearly wrong, but between views none of which can be reasonably rejected.[28] In the face of such disagreements, deliberative democrats should practice the economy of moral disagreement described earlier.

But economizing on moral disagreement does not eliminate it. Consider the debate on homosexual unions.[29] In the spirit of moral economizing, the state would seek a compromise: it would grant legal recognition to both homosexual and heterosexual unions, giving the same legal rights to partners of both kinds of union. This recognition would respect the principles of nondiscrimination and civic equality. At the same time, the state would not require religious associations to recognize either homosexual or heterosexual unions. Such tolerance would respect freedom of religious association as well as the right to argue, whether on a religious basis or not, that marriage should be a union of only men and women and that homosexual acts are sinful. Some citizens would want the law to require that *all* associations not discriminate. Others would continue to defend the freedom of private associations to discriminate, although they themselves might not oppose homosexual unions. And still others would insist that the state should legally recognize homosexual unions as marriages in every respect including by name.

Because reasonable differences will persist, democratic governments and their citizens should learn from the way they are expressed and dealt with. By their nature, reasonable differences contain partial understandings. Each alone is likely to be mistaken if taken comprehensively, all together are likely to be incoherent if taken completely, but all together are likely to be instructive if taken partially. A democracy can govern effectively and prosper morally if its citizens seek to clarify and narrow their deliberative disagreements without giving up their core moral commitments. This is the pluralist hope. It is, in our view, both more charitable and more realistic than the pursuit of the comprehensive common good that consensus democrats favor.

How Far Should Deliberative Democracy Reach?

Deliberative democrats disagree about the scope of deliberation— about how far it should extend popularly, domestically, and internationally. We take a more expansive view of this scope than do some theorists. We accept that most democratic decisions are made by representatives, but would encourage more of those forms of popular participation that increase the quality of deliberation or the fairness of representation. We also believe that some of the institutions of civil society as well as those of government should be more deliberative, and that deliberation should have a more prominent role in international politics.

Representative or Participatory?

The ideal of a society of free and equal citizens does not call on everyone to spend a great amount of time participating in politics. Nor does it require that citizens make all the important political decisions themselves. Most deliberative democrats therefore do not insist that ordinary citizens regularly take part in public deliberations, and most favor some form of representative democracy. On these versions of the theory, citizens rely on their representatives to do their deliberating for them, but representatives are expected not only to deliberate among themselves but also to listen to and communicate with their constituents, who in turn should have many opportunities to hold them accountable. The advantage is that the deliberation by leaders who have been tested by experience (if only by political campaigns) is likely to be more informed, effective, and relevant (if not more sophisticated). The disadvantage is that most citizens become mere spectators; they participate in the deliberation only vicariously. Moreover, and perhaps most critically, representative democracy places a very high premium on citizens' holding their representatives accountable. To the extent that they fail to do so, or are prevented from doing so, their representatives may fail to act responsibly, or even honestly.

Some deliberative democrats therefore favor a more participatory form of government.[30] They argue that more direct participation by ordinary citizens in policy-making is the best or only way to secure many of the moral values (such as mutual respect) that deliberative democracy promises. Greater participation not only gives more citizens the chance to enjoy the benefits of taking part in deliberation, it also can help develop the virtues of citizenship, encouraging citizens to consider political issues in a more public-spirited mode.

The disadvantages of direct democracy, however, are both practical and ethical. The obvious practical objection is that because of the large number of citizens in modern democracies, the advantages of direct democracy can be realized only in local units or subunits in the political system. Moreover, there is simply not enough time for most citizens to participate directly, beyond voting, in any political forum that includes more than a few hundred people. There are also distinct if less obvious ethical disadvantages to direct democracy. Decision-making by the direct assembly of all citizens may not yield either the best laws and public policies or the best deliberative justifications for those laws and public policies.[31] Democratically elected and accountable representatives of citizens may be better deliberators, and are likely to be democratically recognized as such. Moreover, for most people, the freedom not to spend a major part of one's time deliberating about politics is part of what it means to live the life of a free citizen.

We find both the practical and ethical arguments against direct democracy compelling for most cases of decision-making at the national level. Nevertheless, we also believe that in some forums it may be possible to combine some of the advantages of direct deliberative democracy with those of representation. James Fishkin's proposal for deliberative polling—which assembles a random sampling of citizens to discuss policy positions of competing candidates—offers such a way of partially reconciling the deliberative value of direct participation with the necessities of representative democracy in modern society.[32] Fishkin's procedure is no more intrusive than ordinary jury duty, and much more educative than ordinary political campaigns. It can benefit both the citizens and the candidates who take part, as well as those who look on, more than the conventional forms of electoral politics do.

Government or Civil Society?

To what institutions and associations within a democracy should deliberation apply? Deliberative democrats generally agree that its demands extend to those governmental institutions that are

31

responsible for the basic laws that bind people, but they disagree about whether the same deliberative principles also apply outside of these governmental institutions, to civil society more generally.

In his influential statement of the theory of deliberative democracy, Habermas requires deliberation only in those institutions that are core structures of a constitutionally organized democracy.[33] Other deliberative democrats, such as Joshua Cohen and Jane Mansbridge, suggest that deliberation should also take place within a far wider range of political and civic associations, including corporations and labor unions, professional and residential associations, and even families and friendship circles.[34]

If deliberation aims to achieve greater consensus and to enable people to live more respectfully with ongoing disagreements, why not extend it throughout a society rather than limit it only to some governmental institutions? Deliberative democrats like Habermas offer two reasons for the limitation. First, the demands of deliberation cannot be generally applied even to all governmental institutions. As long as legislatures are authorized to regulate other political institutions consistently with constitutional values, they may rightly decide that certain parts of the government, such as executive agencies, should not be made to engage in public deliberation. One legitimate outcome of legislative deliberation is to affirm that certain constitutional values, such as privacy, sometimes take precedence over public deliberation when the two conflict. The American public does not have a right to know the contents of letters sent by our military officers in Iraq to their family members, even if the letters might reveal information that would be relevant to our understanding of the conduct of the war. Governmental as well as nongovernmental institutions that protect familial privacy therefore should not be forced to deliberate publicly over whether to continue to do so, especially in circumstances, like wartime, when pressures to violate basic rights of privacy are great. Citizens may challenge the lack of public deliberation over some matters by protesting to their legislative representatives or by bringing a case to court. But citizens cannot simply claim that all institutions, whatever their purposes, have the same democratic responsibility to engage in public deliberation.

The second reason that some deliberative democrats would not extend the deliberative mandate to all institutions is that such an extension could threaten the freedom of citizens and the associations they choose to form. If citizens are to be free to live as they choose and to experiment with ways of associating, the requirements of deliberation should not seek to regulate all of civil society. A society that is thoroughly deliberative—as a result of governmental mandate—would not be a society of free citizens. To use Habermasian terms, civil society must remain substantially unstructured to allow for free-will formation. In Rawlsian terms, deliberation must not be required beyond what is necessary for citizens to live freely while also respecting the basic liberties and opportunities of their fellow citizens.

Other deliberative theorists believe that these same values of liberty and opportunity imply that deliberation should be extended to civil society. Joshua Cohen argues for "the existence of arenas in which citizens can propose issues for the political agenda and participate in debate about those issues. The extension of such arenas is a public good, and ought to be supported with public money."[35] We agree that deliberation is desirable in many institutions of government and civil society, and especially in those institutions that deal with major failures in civil society. The Truth and Reconciliation Commission (TRC) in South Africa, which we discuss in chapter 6, represents a dramatic example of extending the realm of deliberation beyond conventional governmental institutions. Before, during, and after its formal hearings, the TRC encouraged South African citizens to deliberate in depth about how a newly democratized South Africa should deal with its legacy of apartheid. An important part of the TRC's work concerned the professions in South Africa during the apartheid era—the failures of doctors, lawyers, and psychologists to live up to the standards of their own professions, as well as the requirements of the law. The TRC is a striking example of an institution that bridges state and civil society.

Corporations are another, quite different, example of an institution that should be subject to more deliberation. For citizens to have influence over institutions that affect their basic liberties and opportunities, they need forums within which they can propose and debate issues concerning the basic economic structure of society, over which corporations exert a kind of control that is properly considered political, not only economic. In the wake of recent corporate scandals, including the misuse of pension funds, stock options, and compensation packages for corporate executives, shareholder organizations have called for more deliberation in the bodies that oversee management and boards. The "shareholders dialogue" movement spans the realms of government and civil society by insisting on more public deliberation in both legislatures and corporate boardrooms about the governance, environmental performance, workplace conditions, and investments of large companies.[36] Deliberations between shareholders and corporate management are likely to be more effective than simply voting on formal resolutions, which are not binding on companies. One of the most active shareholder groups in the United States, the Interfaith Center for Corporate Responsibility, files shareholder resolutions but then insists on engaging in a continuing deliberation with management. Shareholder control, even if it becomes more deliberative than it has been, cannot substitute for governmental regulation, since shareholders do not necessarily pursue the public interest. But more robust shareholder participation, more genuine deliberation in corporate governance, could help corporations avoid the increase in governmental regulation that they fear, and could in any case advance the aims of deliberative democracy for the society as a whole.

The argument for extending deliberation to corporations, whose decisions significantly affect people's basic liberties and opportunities in the society, does not necessarily apply to institutions and associations whose purposes are less public and whose effects are less far-reaching. Because deliberative democracy seeks to justify only decisions that collectively bind people, decisions in truly voluntary associations should be less subject to its demands. Politicians, professionals, and corporate officials who have power over other people should be held to publicly defensible standards. In more personal and more voluntary relationships, people should be freer to follow their own distinctive callings. In many voluntary associations, including churches and synagogues, colleges and universities, deliberation still may be desirable even if it should not be externally mandated. But generally, the less the aims of institutions and associations in civil society coincide with those of ordinary politics, the less subject they should be to the force of deliberative principles. Absent some special showing that their decisions directly affect the basic liberties or opportunities of citizens, voluntary associations should be free from any state-imposed requirement to deliberate.

Since deliberation takes time and can create more controversy than it quells, why do deliberative democrats consider it desirable at all in associations where it should not be politically mandated? Are they too much enamored of political talk and too little appreciative of individual freedom and cultural difference? Because most citizens live most of their lives in civil society outside of conventional politics, deliberative theories seek to structure civil society so as to better equip citizens to deliberate in politics. Because deliberative politics works best when citizens do not experience it as an alien activity, some substantial continuity between everyday and political life is desirable. As democratic theorists have long recognized, democracy cannot thrive without a well-educated citizenry. An important part of democratic education is learning how to deliberate well enough to be able to hold representatives accountable. Without a civil society that provides rehearsal space for political deliberation, citizens are less likely to be politically effective.

Because the school system in a democracy appropriately aims to prepare children to become free and equal citizens, it constitutes one of the most important sites of rehearsals for deliberation. It is therefore properly subject to political mandate.[37] Publicly supported and publicly accredited schools should teach future citizens the knowledge and skills needed for democratic deliberation. Much of the same knowledge (understanding of political systems, world history, and economics) and skills (literacy, numeracy, and critical thinking) is also what children need to become effective citizens in today's world.

If schools do not equip children to deliberate, other institutions are not likely to do so. Families are appropriately protected from intrusive political regulation by rights of privacy. The other set of institutions that dominate many people's lives—consisting of the mass media, most prominently television—is among the most unfriendly to deliberation. The media teach consumerism far more more effectively than deliberation. And the potential that some democrats have seen for the internet so far has not been realized.[38] In the most common forms of surfing and posting on the internet, citizens have both less need and less incentive to seek out sites and groups that embrace a broad range of interests and bring together a wide range of perspectives, as genuine deliberation requires. Furthermore, most of the activity on the internet is not political but rather related to entertainment, shopping, travel, sex, and personal relationships.[39]

Domestic or International?

In the modern world, many decisions that a government makes, such as a decision to go to war, obviously affect many people other than its own citizens. It would therefore seem that a theory such as deliberative democracy, which emphasizes the need to justify decisions to people who have to live with the consequences of collective decisions, would extend its requirements to the international arena. Yet most theorists of deliberative democracy apply its principles exclusively to domestic systems of government.[40]

These domestic theorists offer a sensible, practical reason for limiting the reach of deliberative democracy—essentially the reason why most democratic theorists focus their theories on one society at a time. As difficult as it is to solve the problem of disagreement in a single society within a shared legal framework, it is far harder to achieve a justifiable consensus or mutual respect in the even more diverse international sphere, with its many contentious states and its lack of authoritative overarching institutions.

Democratic theorists also give an ethical reason for this limit, one that can be based on the value of reciprocity: citizens who are subject to the duties of citizenship, such as military service and taxation, have the primary right to justification from one another and their accountable representatives.

In our increasingly interdependent world, however, the practical and ethical arguments for confining deliberative democracy to the internal politics of single societies can go only so far. Some deliberative democrats therefore take a more cosmopolitan position. They point out that the differences between domestic and international society are often exaggerated. Many domestic societies are multicultural, and many lack stable legal frameworks. International law has become more effective in recent years, and international institutions have had more influence than many expected. Deliberative democracy, in any case, is not intended to be a description of current political reality. It is an aspirational ideal. (The ideal should of course have some grounding in reality: we suggest later some trends and institutions that offer some indication that the ideal is not entirely utopian.)

The ethical argument for limiting deliberative democracy to particular states may be correct for a wide range of domestic decisions, such as policies on taxation, education, and welfare, but is less obviously correct for other decisions, such as policies on war, trade, immigration, and economic development, which significantly and directly affect people in other countries at least as much as they affect citizens themselves. The decision to go to war against Iraq affected Iraqis more than Americans. Although deliberative democracy, strictly speaking, requires only that justifications be given to citizens who are bound by the decisions, the citizens of foreign countries are no less, and often even more, constrained to accept the consequences of the decisions than are the citizens who are legally bound by them. On these issues, the distinction between being bound and being significantly affected begins to erode.

To the extent that public officials in all democracies accept the burden of providing justifications to those who are significantly affected by their decisions, foreigners become what we call moral constituents even if they are not electoral constituents. On grounds of reciprocity, public officials may ignore the welfare of foreigners only for reasons that foreigners could also accept. In this respect, foreigners stand under the protection of reciprocity. This implication of deliberative accountability means that there are likely to be some policies that are acceptable to citizens but to which some foreigners may reasonably object. Iraqi civilians did not have any claim on Americans to provide health care on an ongoing basis before the United States overthrew the Iraqi regime and occupied the country. But after the war many Iraqis may justifiably object if the United States does not provide health care, at least to those who are victims of the war. And Iraqis may have even stronger claims to continuing assistance. They are making claims, after all, against an invading country that justified its decision for war partly on the basis of the benefits it would bring to the Iraqi people. But even the weaker claim is sufficient to establish that a deliberative democracy that takes reciprocity seriously should take into account moral and not merely electoral constituents.

A public official who appeals to the welfare of Iraqis, even for the purpose of justifying a war, is already acknowledging these individuals as his moral constituents. This kind of appeal, if made in good faith, at least brings citizens of foreign nations into the moral framework of decision-makers. It recognizes the broader scope of deliberative accountability, but it is not sufficient. Recognizing foreigners as moral constituents whose claims should be considered in the deliberative process is not yet recognizing the importance of including them in the actual deliberations. The reason that they should be included in some way in the actual deliberations is simply that without responding to their views, their "representatives" are less likely to know whether their welfare is being promoted. If others do not have a voice in the making of a decision, it is too easy to assume that our decision will benefit them, especially if the decision also benefits us.

If foreigners cannot actually participate in our elections and legislatures, they could still exercise some influence over our decisions if our public officials were to some degree more accountable in international forums. Such accountability is difficult to achieve, and is in some respects rightly resisted in the national interest. But in the current world, it cannot credibly be denied that domestic governments and multinational corporations often exercise the kind of political power that calls for some greater degree of public accountability on an international level. Strengthening institutions like the United Nations and the European Union, as well as some of the non-governmental associations in international civil society, could provide a measure of accountability, or at least a surrogate for it, that is now lacking.

A conception of deliberative democracy that takes a more cosmopolitan perspective asks whether these international institutions on balance aid or impede taking the claims of moral constituents into account in political decision-making. It recommends that we try to make international institutions more deliberative, and that to the extent that they are, nations should give them greater respect. It also favors domestic forums in which public officials speak for the ordinary citizens of foreign nations, presenting their claims and responding to counterclaims. The purpose of such forums, both international and domestic, is to inform citizens and policy-makers alike of the justifiable claims of noncitizens when countries are considering policies that significantly affect noncitizens.

Since the success of democratic accountability depends on the moral capacities of citizens and public officials, elected representatives cannot champion the cause of moral constituents for long without winning the support of their electoral constituents. The more closely the perspectives of electoral constituents track those of moral constituents, the more nearly the deliberative principle of reciprocity can be realized. Although noncitizens may not have the same full claim as citizens on domestic decision-making, they have some substantial claim on major policies that directly affect their lives and basic welfare. In this respect and to this extent, deliberative democracy should promote the globalization of deliberation.

How Can Deliberative Democrats Respond to Theoretical Objections?

The answer to the question "What does deliberative democracy mean?" remains incomplete without a response to the critics of deliberative democracy. Most of the criticisms brought against it are intended to apply to all of its versions, not only the one we have defended here (and in *Democracy and Disagreement*). Some critics question the desirability of the theory itself. They challenge deliberative democracy's fundamental aim of justifying laws on the basis of principles that citizens who are trying to find fair terms of cooperation can reasonably accept. Others would accept the fundamental aim in theory, but deny that it is feasible in practice. In this section we consider the theoretical objections, and in the next section the practical objections.

The Priority of Justice

One of the most common objections to the theory of deliberative democracy is that it sacrifices justice for the sake of democracy. This objection is leveled most forcefully against purely procedural forms of deliberative democracy. In that respect, we have already answered the objection by showing that the proper conception of deliberative democracy goes beyond process. But the objection persists in more subtle forms.

Even those forms of deliberative democracy that include substantive principles (such as justice) still hold that these principles must be interpreted, and conflicts among them resolved, in the deliberative process. These forms of the theory do not exclude justice, but neither do they give it any special status or priority over the process itself. Consequently, the deliberative process can produce results that are unjust. The critic of deliberative democracy argues that however valuable deliberation may be, it should not take precedence over just outcomes. Assume that the deliberative process leading to the decision to go to war against Iraq was fully fair. Does the fair process justify the decision to go to war? Why should deliberative democrats who oppose the war think they have sufficient reason to accept it simply because it resulted from a deliberative process? The opponents of the war may value the benefits of deliberation, but they may disvalue the costs of war more. They would claim that in cases of this kind, where the stakes are high and the answer clear, democracy should defer to justice.

Deliberative democratic theory does not deny that justice should sometimes take priority over deliberation. It suggests that deliberation is generally the best way to arrive at just decisions, or, more accurately, the least unsatisfactory. The justice of the war, like that of many other decisions, is contestable. People of good faith on both sides question the justice of the means and ends of the war, as well as the reasons given to justify the means and ends. Those who are certain that justice is on their side should at least recognize that imposing this view on others requires a further step: trying to persuade those others that there are good reasons for this view.

Suppose, the critic of the war says, that the United States had decided against invading Iraq—but without any deliberation. Would not that outcome have been preferable? Such counterfactual examples support an objection against deliberative democracy only if just outcomes would otherwise have been blocked by deliberation. A just outcome produced without deliberation is not wrong, only less justifiable than it could have been. This example and others like it do not constitute a criticism of the use of deliberation if, as seems likely, the Bush administration would have decided to go to war anyway, only sooner and with less extensive public scrutiny of its reasons, had less deliberation taken place. Deliberative democrats do not claim that deliberation is a panacea, that it can simply turn bad outcomes into good ones, only that it is better than its alternatives.

In the face of controversy about what justice itself entails, deliberative democrats ask citizens to engage with one another under conditions that manifest mutual respect, and with the aim of finding terms of fair cooperation. Deliberative democracy gives justice priority when citizens have good reason to know what justice requires, but they do not acquire sufficient reason to believe they

41

know what it requires for society as a whole without having engaged in reasoned deliberation with their fellow citizens.

The Circularity of Justice

But what if, as another criticism suggests, the conditions under which citizens deliberate about the meaning of justice are themselves unjust? Consider again the deliberation that attended the decision to go to war against Iraq. It took place under conditions that fall short of what justice requires. Gross inequalities of political power and economic wealth, great discrepancies in access to the media, and vast differences in control of information give some people much more power than others in the deliberative forum, even if the deliberation itself otherwise meets the high standards that the theory requires. The problem is not simply that deliberative theory may not be realized (that is a practical objection), but that determining the substantive justice of a particular decision depends on establishing a just process, which in turn depends on determining the substantive justice of the process.

The apparent circularity here is not a defect of deliberative democracy but rather one of its virtues. Deliberative democracy recognizes that the principles of procedural justice are often as contestable as the principles of substantive justice. As we suggested earlier, there is in democratic theory no justification for giving priority to one kind of justice over another, either in general or in advance. But the force of the objection is reduced when we observe that deliberative theory itself has the capacity to question the background conditions, and to show why its own deliberative processes may therefore have produced unjust outcomes. Again, its provisionality furnishes the key response to such objections.

Even under unjust conditions, deliberation can make a more positive contribution to the elimination of injustice than can the alternative processes. When prevailing injustices primarily benefit a dominant social group, deliberation brings this deficiency to public attention. Deliberation is a more promising way of dealing with injustice than the usually available alternatives, such as decision-making by political elites (who are often the source of the problem) or bargaining among interest groups (which usually reproduce the prevailing inequalities). The power of reason is less directly tied to the existing distribution of power, and therefore has the potential to challenge it.

The theory of deliberative democracy does not always in all circumstances demand the practice of deliberation. The best means of promoting deliberative democracy in the future may sometimes require refraining from deliberation in the present, for example, to ensure a timely and necessary life-saving response to a crisis. But under these nonideal conditions, both deliberative democrats and their critics can reasonably be asked to propose alternatives to deliberation. Whatever alternatives they propose, we should remember, need to be justified to their fellow citizens. To justify the nondeliberative alternatives, they need to engage in deliberation.

The Redundancy of Deliberation

Some critics of deliberative democracy go further. They argue that deliberation is not necessary at all in justifying political decisions. They do not believe that the process of justifying an outcome to the people who are bound by it contributes anything of significance to its legitimacy or justice. Joseph Raz argues that decisions and laws have all the authority they need if they are right or just.[41] They need no further justification of the sort that deliberative democrats require. A law is either right or wrong, period. If it is right, then it does not need to be justified to anyone. If it is wrong, then it cannot be justified to anyone. Similarly, Raz might say that if a law is partly right and partly wrong, this has nothing to do with whether it can be shown to be so to the people who are bound by it, but who may be morally mistaken about its justice.

Despite his disdain for public justification, Raz does not really deny that deliberation may be useful in arriving at better (more just) outcomes in politics. Raz and deliberative democrats can agree that to the extent that deliberation helps decision-makers make better decisions than they would have otherwise made, it has value. Raz's critique has a point only when deliberation does not serve the aim of reaching better decisions. The point, evidently, is that, at least in theory, knowing the right answer does not depend on decision-makers' deliberating with anyone, let alone doing so in public. And the point is surely valid with respect to some moral claims. Consider the principle of truth-telling. If honesty is truly the best policy, public officials need not publicly deliberate about whether it is the best policy to know that it is. An American president respecting the principle would give his honest reasons for going to war against Iraq. Although there are some occasions on which the principle should be overridden, no amount of deliberation could turn the principle that honesty is the best policy on its head.

This critique proves both too little and too much. It proves too little because although public officials may believe that honesty is the best policy, they may be sorely tempted in any given situation to subordinate this belief to political expediency. The requirement that officials should publicly justify their decisions can help them resist this temptation. The critique proves too much by generalizing a conclusion that may be valid in personal morality and applying it to political morality where it is not. In personal morality (or in moral theory) we may not need to justify our decisions to anyone to know they are right. But in political morality decision-makers have a further moral obligation, which is what deliberative democracy seeks to capture in its demand for public justification. It is not enough for an American president, who claims to be acting in the interests of his country and the entire world, to know in his heart that he is right. His electoral and moral constituents may reasonably ask to know his reasons for thinking he is right. It is not enough for people who exercise power over others to think they know in their hearts they are right, because (1) they may in fact be wrong; (2) others cannot effectively judge whether the power holders are right or wrong if they do not subject their reasons to public scrutiny; and (3) others may reasonably regard them as less trustworthy if they do not offer their reasons publicly.

The need for justification extends beyond any single decision. Any flaws in a public official's principles or their application are more likely to come to light and be corrected if they are subject to broad public scrutiny over time. The demands for justification that persisted after the decision to go to war against Iraq illustrate the need for continuing deliberation. Even when prospective accountability fails, retrospective accountability may contribute to better decision-making in the future, by calling a public official to critical account after the fact.

There are also expressive reasons for ongoing public justification. Deliberation understood as public justification depends on a value—civic freedom, which is implied by reciprocity in politics— that the critics themselves accept but the political implications of which they fail to pursue. Civic freedom entails the effective liberty to affirm or deny the reasoning of one's representatives. Citizens cannot exercise this liberty unless officials justify their actions, and respond to criticism. Officials act in the name of citizens who are owed a good-faith account of the officials' reasons for action, not just once and for all, but over time. The refusal at any given time to offer fellow citizens an account may reflect more pressing public concerns or a momentary lapse of judgment, but a pattern of refusal demonstrates a lack of respect for their public standing as citizens, as well as the moral and political agency that attends this standing in a democracy. The failure to support the iteration of deliberation is therefore far more significant than a singular suspension or lapse.

If representatives refuse to subject their decisions to public deliberation (either prospectively or retrospectively), then they have no legitimate basis for claiming to the citizens on whose behalf they are acting that their actions are right. And in so behaving, they are also treating those over whom they exercise power as objects of paternalistic legislation rather than as democratic citizens to whom they owe an honest account of their actions. This defense of deliberation implies that an important part of a political decision's being right is that it is actually justified to the people who not only are bound by it but are the source of its political authority. Another implication of this defense is that the difference between justice and legitimacy is not as sharp in collective decision-making that binds people as it may be in other contexts.

The Primacy of Power

Another theoretical critique of deliberative democracy goes still further: it gives power priority over both justice and deliberation. Stanley Fish argues that the demand for justification is misguided because it presupposes a shared understanding of what counts as a good reason.[42] There is no such shared understanding, especially in politics. Distinguishing good from bad (or better from worse) reasons in politics amounts to no more than expressing one's personal opinion or a group's prejudices.

In defending the need to give reasons to justify laws and public policies, deliberative democrats are not only misguided, according to Fish, they are disingenuous. What they really are doing is presenting their personal preferences in the guise of giving morally objective reasons. As evidence for his critique, Fish suggests that in *Democracy and Disagreement* Gutmann and Thompson end up rationalizing their own liberal egalitarian policy preferences as an integral part of their (supposedly correct) theory of deliberative democracy. Giving reasons is the chief way academics exercise power in democratic politics. All the talk about deliberation, like deliberation itself, is merely a cover for power politics. Deliberative democrats themselves may not be especially powerful in achieving their goals in the contemporary political arena, where a "deliberative deficit" persists and liberal egalitarian agendas rarely prevail. But deliberative democrats do damage nonetheless. To the extent that they make politics more deliberative, they also make decisions and policies seem more moral when they are not.

Fish and other critics who press similar objections have a point. Like other worthy methods of political decision-making, deliberation can also be used cynically. It can serve as a cover for the exercise of power politics. And it is not a substitute for the exercise of other forms of power in politics. But the critics ignore one of the most effective antidotes to both the misuse of deliberation and the neglect of desirable forms of power politics—the use of deliberation itself to publicly expose the unjustified exercise of political power. Deliberation can expose injustices by distinguishing between, on the one hand, claims that rationalize undemocratic or illiberal ends and, on the other, those that support the equal liberty, opportunity, and civic equality of individuals.

Fish seems to suggest that there is no way to distinguish between justified and unjustified exercises of political power. Does he really think that the best reasons for extending equal rights to all human beings regardless of skin color are no better than those offered for slavery and racial discrimination? If he holds that the arguments for civic equality and racial inferiority are equally defensible, then his critique of deliberative democracy applies to all forms of democracy. He seems to have put democracy on the same moral footing as apartheid, authoritarianism, and fascism. If Fish acknowledges that racial inferiority is not as defensible as civic equality, then his critique undermines itself. Some justifications turn out to be better than others, independently of the political power that may support them, or the self-interests and group interests that may motivate them. The effort to debunk all distinctions between better and worse arguments is ultimately self-defeating, because it can succeed only if its reasons are right. But that is precisely the kind of claim that the critic insists on discrediting.

A critique that reduces reasons to power politics can succeed only by deception. The critic's listeners will be convinced by his arguments only to the extent that they misunderstand him to be presenting reasonable arguments, which he must deny if he is being truthful. On the one hand, if he is being deceptive, no one has any acceptable reason to give his arguments any credence. On the other hand, if he is being truthful, then no one has any acceptable reason to think his arguments are anything more than covers for asserting his self-interest. Once people recognize that his rules of argument authorize him to say anything that helps him win, and that winning is merely a matter of causing people to accept his views (whatever they happen to be), his arguments dissolve into self-assertion. This kind of self-assertion may be common enough in politics, but it is not the kind of politics that most democrats wish to encourage. Anyone who would defend this kind of politics would need to present arguments that could be accepted by his fellow citizens. If he does so, he enters willy-nilly into the forums of deliberative democracy, and falls under its obligations of reasonable argument.

How Can Deliberative Democrats
Respond to Practical Objections?

One can accept the fundamental aim of justifying the decisions that leaders make on behalf of others, and agree that deliberation is desirable in a political context where citizens are free and equal, but still object to the ways in which deliberation is manifested in practice.

Deliberative Biases

Deliberative democracy, as we have seen, is about more than the process of deliberation alone. It is also about substantive standards of free and equal citizenship, and about the background conditions of free and equal citizenship that deliberation needs if it is to function as well as it can. Because the conditions of actual democratic politics fall short of these standards, even theorists who are attracted to the goals of deliberative democracy can criticize it for producing unjust outcomes under current conditions, and indeed all conditions likely to be realized in the foreseeable future. When power is distributed unequally and when money substantially affects who has access to the deliberative forum, the results of deliberation in practice are likely to reflect these inequalities, and therefore lead, in many cases, to unjust outcomes.

But even under these conditions deliberative democracy is its own best critic. Here again the theory of deliberative democracy challenges the practice of deliberative democracy. Deliberative democracy itself exposes the exclusionary biases in democratic practice that undermine the conditions of civic equality that its principles defend. To the extent that the least advantaged are excluded because they are too poor to have equal access to the political media, the principles of deliberative democracy support an effective critique of this unfairness.

Consider the inequality of campaign financing in the United States. Campaign contributions, which come disproportionately from wealthy citizens and well-organized groups, influence who runs for office, who is elected, and the policies that successful candidates support. The system of financing campaigns through private contributions disadvantages already disadvantaged citizens. Public financing of campaigns could ameliorate this problem, and so—even more surely—would a fairer distribution of income and wealth. Notice that this kind of critique emanates from deliberative democratic theory itself. It is fully consistent with both the spirit and the principles of the theory.

The policies that would be required to change these background inequalities, and therefore decrease the bias of democratic deliberation, are not likely to be supported by a power politics that favors the wealthiest individuals, the most powerful groups, and their representatives. Representatives who win election through the influence of money are not likely to support a reform that could spell their own political demise. Any successful strategy for arriving at a justifiable policy with regard to campaign financing needs to make the moral case against money buying political power. The light that extensive public deliberation can shine on the legislature may under some circumstances make some legislators take these moral arguments seriously. But it may be necessary and ultimately more effective to delegate authority for governing the campaign finance system to an independent commission, one that is not controlled by the politicians and parties whose future is at stake in any reform.[43] Although deliberative democratic theory is not committed to any particular institutional reform of this kind, it does call for changes that would eliminate, as far as possible, those biases in the political process (including deliberative forums) that derive from unequal wealth and entrenched power.

Some critics object that deliberative practices are biased in a different way. They suggest that deliberative competency, along with the style and standards of deliberative reasoning, further disadvantages already disadvantaged citizens.[44] These critics appear to assume that the educational disadvantages suffered by members of marginalized groups have diminished their capacity for deliberation, both as participants and as spectators. Deliberative democrats themselves object to these educational disadvantages, and join with the critics in seeking to change them. But in the meantime, does the bias in the system discredit the use of deliberation in seeking a society of greater civic equality? Not if the alternative of power politics is less likely to achieve greater justice. Critics tend to overlook the fact that disadvantaged groups usually manage to find representatives from within their own ranks who are as effective at articulating their interests and ideals as the representatives put forward by established groups. Such leaders do not have to be as gifted as Martin Luther King, Jr., to promote the cause of justice for the disadvantaged. Suffering the effects of discrimination and other forms of injustice often produces leaders who are more committed, more insightful, and more charismatic than leaders of privileged groups in society.

The lack of political success of marginalized groups does not stem from a lack of deliberative competency, but rather from a lack of power. To the extent that the political struggles take place on the basis of deliberation rather than power, they are more evenly matched. Because moral appeals are the weapon of the weak, a deliberative playing field is more nearly level. As we noted earlier, compared to bargaining or other purely aggregative methods of politics, deliberation can diminish the discriminatory effects of class, race, and gender inequalities that rightly trouble critics.

Is the style of argument that deliberative democracy requires biased in favor of the advantaged? Groups intent on challenging the status quo do not usually engage in the cool reason-giving that deliberative democracy seems to favor. Seeking to mobilize their own supporters or to gain public attention, they often take extreme positions, and make heated appeals. They are more likely to use passion than reason. And for good reason: emotional rhetoric is often more effective than rational syllogism.

But the critics assume a dichotomy between passion and reason that deliberative democracy need not and should not accept. They also imply that members (or representatives) of disadvantaged groups are less reasonable in their appeals than their more advantaged counterparts. The assumption and implication are misleading. As a generalization, it would be hard to show that defenders of the disadvantaged have been less reasonable in presenting their arguments than defenders of the status quo. Deliberative standards such as being truthful and offering moral reasons are easier to satisfy when criticizing distributive injustices than when defending them. Supporters of the status quo, moreover, show no reluctance to use passionate appeals.

Deliberative democrats should recognize that in the political arena passionate rhetoric can be as justifiable as logical demonstration. Those who speak on behalf of the disadvantaged can ill afford to ignore the need to be effective. Theorists as well as politicians, at least since the days of Athenian politics and Aristotelian rhetoric, have recognized the legitimacy of modes of persuasion in politics that combine reason and passion. Furthermore, rhetoric may properly have to tip toward passion in some circumstances. Some issues cannot even reach the political agenda unless some citizens are willing to act with passion, making statements and declarations rather than developing arguments and responses. When nondeliberative politics—antiwar marches, sit-ins, and workers' strikes—are necessary to achieve deliberative ends, deliberative theory consistently suspends its requirements for deliberation. We should also observe that these activities often provoke more deliberation than would otherwise occur. But even when they do not, they can be justified if they lead to future occasions for deliberative criticism of injustice.

Another charge of bias against deliberative democrats is that their standards of public reason discriminate against certain kinds of beliefs, particularly against certain religious perspectives. The requirement that reasons be mutually acceptable and generally accessible is not morally neutral. No standard of reasoning could be. The critical question must be whether deliberative standards are unfair. They are not legally binding and therefore do not restrict anyone's right of free speech, but it is alleged that they make it harder for some citizens (those with certain religious views) to justify the decisions and policies they favor.

51

Consider the ongoing debate in the United States over legalizing and funding the use of stem cells from cloned human embryos for biomedical research. The charge of bias implies that all arguments for and against legalizing and funding should be considered equally appropriate. In contrast, deliberative democrats hold that arguments should be considered more or less appropriate bases for legal action depending on their mutual acceptability and general accessibility. The report issued by the President's Commission for Bioethics in July 2002 is instructive in this regard.[45] All Commission members supported a ban on cloning to produce children, but they divided over whether cloning for biomedical research should be permitted and publicly funded. A ten-member majority favored a qualified ban on some research, while a seven-member minority opposed it. Although the Commission members had different religious backgrounds and beliefs, neither the majority nor the minority invoked religious reasons that were not accessible to other members. The moral issues considered by both sides—the status of the cloned embryo, harm to society, and obligations to those who are suffering— were accessible not only to members but to citizens.

Despite its extensive deliberations, the Commission could not formulate a set of recommendations that were mutually acceptable to all. Yet mutual acceptability, not merely accessibility, is an aim of the public reason that deliberative democracy favors. Critics may fault deliberative democracy for falling short of its aspiration to find a set of mutually acceptable recommendations in this case. But it would be misleading to infer from this criticism that we should reject the standards of public reason. Because of the wide range of beliefs found in every democratic society, it would be unrealistic to expect agreement on every controversial moral issue. Cloning stem cells is a salient issue over which public agreement in the United States is probably not yet possible. But the continuing effort to present reasons that are accessible, with the aim of reaching conclusions that are acceptable, can contribute to moral progress.

The President's Commission not only aimed at agreement, but also economized on its disagreements. Both sides appealed to principles—such as respect for human life and relief of human suffering—that any citizen who is trying to find fair terms of cooper-ation could reasonably accept. The members disagreed on what con-stitutes a fully human life, and therefore on how to compare the im-portance of relieving human suffering to the value of preserving the life of a human embryo. They could not agree on the application of these principles in the case of therapeutic research at hand. But be-cause both the majority and minority explicitly accepted some com-mon principles, they could reach agreement on the recommendation against cloning, and, equally important, they could find respectful ways of continuing the public discussion on the issues on which they may never reach agreement, and on related issues on which they stand a better chance of reaching agreement in the future.

Undesirable Consequences

Even if deliberative democracy could be shown to be no more biased in practice than other forms of democracy, some critics worry that it would have other undesirable consequences. They suggest that de-liberative democracy is likely to undermine stability by discounting the legitimate agreements made in the past, and by encouraging un-necessarily contentious and divisive political debate.

Because deliberative democracy opens all principles and practices to challenge on moral terms, it appears to undermine po-litical stability. The need for stability appears to be ignored by a pol-itics that considers each and every principle and practice, including those considered most constitutionally sacred, as constantly open to challenge in the democratic forum. This objection focuses our attention on the flip side of what we earlier described as a virtue of deliberative democracy—providing opportunities to escape the dead hand of majorities and (in some instances) minorities who would impose their wills on the present. Here the concern is that even legitimate and reasonable principles are at risk in a democracy that is in a constant state of deliberative enthusiasm.

This criticism misconstrues the practical implications of provisionality. Deliberative democracy recognizes that constitu-tional rights should be more insulated than ordinary laws, but it

53

does not assume that simply because a claim is a constitutional right it should be completely insulated from deliberation. The degree of institutional insulation that any law should have from democratic deliberation depends on the degree of confidence that people of any particular generation should reasonably have in its justification. The greater their reasonable confidence, the more insulation is justified. Given the protection that slavery and male-only suffrage initially received in the U.S. Constitution, critics of deliberative democracy must at least acknowledge that completely insulating constitutions from change cannot be justified. By allowing for orderly change that takes into account how justified particular laws are, deliberative democracy offers the degree of deference due to the past, but no more.

Other critics worry that deliberation exacerbates the fractious and potentially extremist potential of a democratic politics, which—especially in the pluralist societies that deliberative democrats accept—should strive for justifiable compromise and convergence as much as possible. Cass Sunstein, a defender of deliberative democracy, draws attention to empirical evidence showing that some deliberative processes polarize "members of a deliberating group [who] predictably move toward a more extreme point."[46] Democrats should not want to encourage a process that promotes extremism.

This polarization effect, however, is not inevitable. It occurs under certain kinds of conditions and not others. The groups that Fishkin assembled for his deliberative opinion polling did not polarize.[47] The differences between the conditions that produce non-polarizing deliberations rather than polarizing deliberations are instructive. Nonpolarizing groups do not begin by voting, are large enough to represent random samples rather than skewed samples of opinions, have moderators who oversee the deliberations to ensure that all perspectives receive a fair hearing, enlist experts to answer questions and clarify matters of fact, and have extensive information available to all participants ahead of time. Participants in deliberative groups that have these characteristics tend not to polarize but rather to find greater common ground than they had before.

Nevertheless, deliberative democrats should recognize that, depending on the moral content of controversy and the available alternatives, convergence is not always to be preferred to polarization. Convergence in acceptance of racial discrimination is not preferable to controversy, even if no one could foresee whether the controversy would lead to more just legislation.

Even when deliberation ends in disagreement, we should recognize that deliberation itself is rarely the root cause of the controversy. If the issues are sufficiently important and deep, as in the case of going to war against Iraq, moral disagreement persists. In that case, suppressing controversy is neither feasible nor desirable. It is likely to erupt even without the encouragement of deliberative democrats, and it is likely to express differences that should be addressed if moral progress is to be possible. Those who wish to suppress controversy are typically those who stand to gain from suppression, and often to gain advantages that they could not justify if they had to defend them in the light of public debate.

Other critics are not so worried about the undesirable consequences described so far, simply because they doubt whether deliberation has any important direct effects at all. But paying so much attention to it may distract theorists, citizens, and politicians from more important activities in political life. Even if deliberation is desirable, it is overrated by deliberative democrats. Compared to other more clearly political activities—organizing, mobilizing, demonstrating, bargaining, lobbying, campaigning, fund-raising, and voting—deliberating does not seem to be a very significant form of political action. Why then do deliberative democrats single it out for such special consideration? They seem to encourage people to spend a great deal of time, if not money, on deliberative activities. This distracts them from other, more useful political activities. Organizing the least advantaged, mobilizing them to vote, and lobbying for reforms that encourage voting are among the many nondeliberative activities that are more likely to produce morally better consequences than calling for more political deliberation.

Michael Walzer, a critic who raises this kind of objection, asks deliberative democrats: "Is this our utopia—a world where political conflict, class struggle, and ethnic and religious differences are all replaced by pure deliberation?"[48] This is not the utopia that any deliberative democrat should defend. Because democracies depend on a wide range of political activities, they also need to assess the relative contributions of those activities to democratic life, and how these practices can be improved. Citizens and their representatives need to assess, for example, the quality of campaigns, their role in the political process, and their relationship to other activities, such as mobilization and political education. Deliberative democrats recommend that these activities be evaluated by deliberative principles and in public forums, not that every political activity itself be deliberative.

Deliberative democrats do not deny the importance of many other kinds of political activities, but they should insist that deliberating is not just another activity on the list. Deliberation provides the means by which the justifiability of the other activities can be determined. Deliberative democracy does not require that all political activities in all places at all times be deliberative. But it does demand that they should be assessed at some time by deliberative principles. Informed by deliberative principles as well as practices, citizens can modify and improve these other activities—making the routines of bargaining, campaigning, voting, and other important political activities more public-spirited in both process and outcome.

Whither Deliberative Democracy?

The future of deliberative democracy depends on meeting two general challenges, one theoretical and one practical. Theoretically, deliberative democrats must recognize the provisional nature not only of democratic deliberation but also of their own theory of democratic deliberation. Both their theory and their practice need to be essentially responsive to change. Practically, deliberative democrats must work not only to make the familiar institutions of democracy more friendly to deliberation but also to extend the scope of deliberation to institutions where it has not previously dared to go. Each of these challenges merits separate discussion.

The Theoretical Challenge

Deliberative democrats should try to ensure that not only the practice but also the theory of democracy they favor is systematically open to challenge. How is it possible to defend principles such as liberty and opportunity as integral to a theory and simultaneously allow for the rejection of these same principles? If deliberative democrats are prepared to take a dynamic view of their own theory, as we have suggested they should, they can regard their principles, not as fixed at any point in time, but as subject to change over time. Not all the theory's principles can be challenged at the same time, but any principle (or several) may be challenged at a particular time by other principles in the theory. The theory in this way contains the means of its own revision.

This self-correcting capacity of deliberative democracy is what we call its provisionality—moral and political. A theory is morally provisional if its principles invite revision in response to new moral insights or empirical discoveries. Many theorists allow for the possibility that their conclusions may be mistaken. But deliberative theorists must be open to the possibility that their substantive principles of democracy may need to be changed. A deliberative theory can become, for example, more or less egalitarian, or more or less libertarian, while still remaining fully deliberative. A deliberative theory can permit challenge to deliberation itself (though not a general denial of the need for justification in politics). In the debate in the British House of Commons about making a new drug available in the National Health Service (see chapter 5), some members in effect argued against further deliberation. They believed that the conclusions of the deliberative body set up to evaluate the new drugs would legitimize the government's refusal to increase the budget for health care, which they believed that justice required. Yet it was in a deliberative forum—the House of Commons—that they raised this objection. It is therefore within the potential of a deliberative process to respond by modifying its own principles.

Deliberative democrats should be committed to regarding their principles as subject to revision not only through moral

57

argument among themselves, but also through moral argument by citizens and their representatives deliberating together in political forums, including school boards, legislatures, and courts. The rationale for this commitment rests on the value of reciprocity. People should be treated not merely as objects of legislation, as passive subjects to be ruled, but as agents who take part in governance, directly or through their representatives, by presenting and responding to reasons that would justify the laws under which they must live together. Decision-makers owe their constituents justifications for the laws that they seek to impose, and they must take seriously the reasons their opponents give. Taking those reasons seriously means that decision-makers must acknowledge the possibility that the reasonable views they reject may be shown to be correct in the future. This acknowledgment has implications not only for the way decision-makers should treat their opponents but also for the way they should regard their own views. It imposes an obligation to continue to test their views, seeking forums in which they can be questioned, and keeping open the possibility of their revision.

A well-known case in which claims of religious freedom were set against public education can illustrate the value of both moral and political provisionality.[49] It shows how the interpretation and implications of a core principle of deliberative democracy—reciprocity—can be subjected to challenge and potential revision. In this case, a court denied the claim of some fundamentalist Christian parents who sought exemptions for their children from the standard reading curriculum in a public school in Tennessee. They claimed that the content of the required textbooks conflicted with their religious convictions.[50] The parents maintained that their children should not be taught to make critical judgments, to use their imaginations, or to exercise choice "in areas where the Bible provides the answer."

We argued that the principle of reciprocity implies that the parents' claim should be rejected. Because the capacity to make critical judgments is a prerequisite for making reciprocal claims, denying future citizens the opportunity to develop that capacity is not consistent with the principle of reciprocity. In a critique of this argument William Galston invokes the very same idea of reciprocity to defend the parents' appeal to the court to exempt their children.[51] Galston imagines the fundamentalist parents saying: "If you believed what I believe . . . you would seek for your child what I am seeking for mine. Moreover, the accommodation I seek is one that I would readily grant, were our positions reversed."[52]

Galston's argument on the parents' behalf is itself based on reciprocity. It recognizes that citizens owe one another mutually justifiable reasons for the laws that they would impose on one another. Because it satisfies the basic principle of reciprocity, Galston's argument is far better than any that the parents or their advocates presented in the actual court case. It is perfectly appropriate in a deliberative process that invites ongoing challenges to public policies. In response to such an argument, the school board could have sought an alternative way of teaching the children the skills and attitudes needed for citizenship—one that could have been consistent with the parents' religious beliefs and also with the state's civic aim of educating future citizens. This kind of search for an alternative, in a deliberative forum, respects the idea of reciprocity.

In contrast, a decision issued by a court to exempt the children would have granted the parents the power, once and for all, to deny these children the opportunities for future citizenship that other children enjoy. Although we do not believe that Galston's argument justifies a court decision in favor of the parents, the fact that he could use the deliberative principle of reciprocity to challenge the conclusions of our deliberative theory shows that the conclusions of deliberative democracy are genuinely provisional, open to revision and reinterpretation in appropriate forums over time.

The Practical Challenge

The future of deliberative democracy also depends on whether its proponents can create and maintain practices and institutions that enable deliberation to work well. Deliberative democrats endorse familiar institutions that support both fair procedures and individual rights.

But they should also recognize that important moral questions— including questions about what constitutes fair procedures and individual rights—cannot be removed from everyday democratic politics. They therefore should support institutions that encourage citizens and public officials to deliberate about their disagreements on these constitutional questions, as well as on ordinary legislation. Citizens and their representatives, not only experts and judges, should attend to the fundamental values of democratic government.

Deliberative institutions also should recognize the provisional nature of principles (and the decisions they justify) by providing mechanisms for regular reconsideration of decisions. Deliberative democrats should thus support reiterative processes in which proposals are modified through a sequence of responses and counterresponses (as in the Oregon case mentioned earlier). They should also seek more flexible procedures for constitutional amendments and more frequent use of devices such as sunset laws that force review of policies.

This openness to change does not mean that deliberative democrats have to favor more frequent voting on laws or officeholders. They should be quite critical of the increasing use of initiatives, referenda, and recall, because these measures generally take place under conditions that are even less deliberative than ordinary elections.[53] The 2003 California gubernatorial recall election exemplifies what is wrong with referenda from a deliberative perspective. The procedure allows hundreds of candidates to gain a place on the recall ballot with almost no prior deliberation by citizens or political parties. The large numbers of candidates and the mixing of two different questions on the ballot—should the governor be recalled? who should replace him?—were bound to produce a chaotic campaign, one that was more confused and demagogic than more usual forms of political debate. Because neither the procedure nor its results could be said to be democratic in the simplest procedural sense (it does not require a majority of the electorate), judicial intervention to correct some of the defects may be called for.

Because deliberative democrats assume that disagreement will persist into the foreseeable future, they seek institutions and policies that enable citizens to live with it on moral terms. Deliberative democrats therefore should defend a wide range of ordinary political phenomena that can facilitate moral accommodation, such as multi-issue cooperation, coalition-building, and political civility. They should also recommend more broad-based political organizations that permit citizens who hold different moral positions on some issues to work together on other causes whose goals they share. For example, a fluid and open party system would be more desirable than a political structure dominated by single-issue groups.

Deliberative democrats, as we indicated earlier, should also favor the extension of deliberative practices into civil society. They should take an interest in the whole range of intermediary institutions—those that act on citizens (such as the media, health-care organizations, professional sports), those in which citizens act (interest groups, private clubs, trade unions, professional associations), as well as those in which they work (corporations, small businesses, government agencies, military service). From a deliberative perspective, the single most important institution outside government is the educational system. To prepare their students for citizenship in a deliberative democracy, schools should aim to develop the capacities of students to understand different perspectives, communicate their understandings to other people, and engage in the give-and-take of moral argument with a view toward making mutually justifiable decisions.

Although most deliberative democrats have concentrated on domestic politics, the pressures of globalization, as we also noted earlier, should encourage them to extend their theory and practice to international forums. Issues as consequential as world poverty, famine, terrorism, AIDS, economic development, and the global environment depend for their resolution on far more cross-national deliberation than can be accomplished within any single set of domestic political institutions. Only after public debate about the problem of AIDS moved from domestic institutions to the World Health Organization, the Global Fund, and UNAIDS did the nations most afflicted by the AIDS epidemic and the nations better situated to help combat the epidemic begin to cooperate to take more effective action, such as changes in policies restricting the distribution of drugs to treat the disease.

Some democratic theorists propose the creation of new global institutions that would constitute a "network of regional and international agencies and assemblies that cut across spatially delimited locales."[54] We agree that some new deliberative forums may be necessary to address global issues, but we also take seriously the concern that multiplying decision-making authorities tends to undermine democratic accountability (an essential condition of deliberative democracy itself). Democratic accountability is at risk in these proposals because most international institutions are undemocratic at their base. The political systems of the majority of the countries whose populations must be represented on issues of global importance remain undemocratic. If the decisions that emanate from these institutions are to be justified to the people whom they bind, then decision-makers at these levels must also take into account their moral constituents, not just their electoral constituents. Where accountability is less, publicity must help fill the gap. The role of communication in supporting deliberation—through the media, the internet, and international exchanges of all kinds—therefore becomes even more important in the international sphere than it is in the domestic sphere.

The prospects of these and other institutional reforms depend on recognizing the need to justify the use of political power to all those who are substantially subject to its dominion. Deliberative democracy is thus more than a procedure. It is a process that requires decision-makers to accept the responsibility of justifying the substance of the decisions they make on behalf of others—their fellow citizens, and at least some of their fellow human beings in the rest of the world. Whether the institutional platform on which public officials stand when they speak is domestic or international, they are responsible for giving mutually accessible and acceptable reasons to the people who have to live with the consequences of their decisions. The content of those reasons matters. The case of the unilateral decision to invade Iraq with which we began stands as a reminder that the actual reasons presented in public deliberation may fall short of what deliberative principles require, and may not produce the outcomes that some deliberative democrats might desire.

But this case should also remind us that deliberative democracy has resources to support continuing challenges to the decisions that leaders make. If citizens and their representatives make better use of those resources, they can create better conditions for the realization of deliberative democracy.

2

Moral Conflict and Political Consensus

When citizens reasonably disagree about the morality of a public policy, on what principles can they agree to conduct their public life? The hope of liberal political theory, and the basis of the most common solution to the problem of moral conflict in a pluralist society, is that citizens can at least agree on principles that would remove decisions about a policy from the political agenda. Liberals typically invoke higher-order principles (such as neutrality or impartiality) that are intended to transcend disagreement on specific policies. These principles purport to determine which issues are appropriate subjects for public policy and which are not. When there is no reasonable basis for resolving the moral conflict on an issue of policy, the principles preclude state action on the issue and leave each citizen free to act, with respect to that issue, on the basis of his or her own morality (to the extent possible without provoking state action). A consensus on these principles thus insulates the political process from fundamental moral conflict.

We want to challenge, at least in part, this familiar liberal way of dealing with moral conflict. The consensus on these higher-order principles that liberals propose is not sufficient to eliminate moral conflict from politics, and a more robust set of principles is necessary to govern the conflict that inevitably and legitimately remains. The higher-order principles that constitute the core of the consensus, we suggest, must permit greater moral disagreement about policy and greater moral agreement on how to disagree about policy.

Two kinds of higher-order principles, corresponding to different purposes that the consensus is supposed to serve, should be distinguished. First, there are what may be called *principles of preclusion*, which serve the more familiar purpose of determining which policies deserve a place on the political agenda, in the sense of being a legitimate subject for legislation. These principles preclude fundamental moral conflict by denying certain reasons their moral standing in the policy-making process. Policies that cannot be justified by the appropriate reasons are precluded, typically by appeal to a written or unwritten constitution. We argue that any justifiable principles of preclusion will dispose of fewer reasons and therefore fewer policies than modern liberals usually assume. Although any adequate principles will not be morally neutral and thus will exclude *some* reasons and policies, they will also open up the political agenda to more moral disagreement than liberal theories usually allow.

Second, there are what may be called *principles of accommodation*, which govern the conduct of the moral disagreement on issues that should reach the political agenda. Liberal theorists have given these principles less attention because they assume that most fundamental moral disagreement is legitimately beyond the scope of governmental action. As long as the principles of preclusion do their job, liberals assume, the principles of accommodation will not have much moral work to do. Procedural principles (such as majority rule) regulate public-policy disputes, and interpersonal principles of minimal moral content (such as toleration) take care of disputes outside the public forum. But if, as we suggest, the principles of preclusion do not preclude so much after all, the principles of accommodation must assume greater importance than they usually have been accorded in liberal theory. We claim that such principles are essential for dealing with the problem of moral disagreement, and that they should go beyond the idea of toleration. They should be understood as resting on the idea of mutual respect, which is a prerequisite of democratic deliberation.

Principles of Preclusion

Religious controversy has traditionally been regarded as the paradigm of moral conflict that does not belong on the political agenda, and it continues to play that role in much recent liberal theory.[1] The assumption is that if the principles of preclusion can banish religious conflict from politics, then they might also dispose of other significant moral conflicts, such as controversies over abortion, pornography, or surrogate parenting. But in its more familiar form the argument for religious toleration does not serve to eliminate even religious conflict from politics. In its Lockean form, the argument for religious toleration can serve this purpose, but the premises of the Lockean argument open up the agenda to many other kinds of moral conflict.

The more familiar, more modern version of the argument for religious toleration assumes a skeptical attitude toward religious belief and requires that the state be neutral toward all religions. It proceeds in three steps. The first step characterizes the nature of the moral conflict: in a pluralist society, citizens disagree about what is the true religion, and even whether there is any true religion at all. There is no rational way, no set of principles or forms of reasoning, that could, even among reasonable people, determine that one particular religion is true (even relatively true for a particular society at a particular time). This establishes the skeptical premise.

The second step is to show that the nature of the conflict requires the state to be neutral or impartial. Since no religion has any rational claim to truth, the state should not favor one religion rather than another, either in the effects of its actions or in its rationale for them. This is the neutrality premise.[2]

The third step is to demonstrate that neutrality implies that the state should not act on religious issues. Any action by the state requires justification, in a way that inaction does not, because action is an exercise of coercion against citizens. Since there is no justification for favoring any religion, neutrality implies inaction. This is the inaction premise. The three premises lead to the conclusion that the state should exclude religious questions from the political agenda. Citizens collectively should tolerate all religions and individually practice their own (or none) as they wish.

Although this is the form of the argument that is supposed to be applied to other issues, as well as religion, it does not work well even for religion. We can see where it goes wrong by comparing it at each step with the Lockean form of the argument for toleration, which though now less familiar is potentially a stronger defense of toleration.

The Lockean argument does not begin with a skeptical premise—and for good reason.[3] The claim that religious truths are unknowable and therefore that no religious party has a right to impose its "truths" on any other proves too much. Many religious citizens could not accept it without abandoning their religious beliefs, or at least without abandoning an important belief about those beliefs—namely, that the beliefs are true. If the only way to establish toleration is to forswear religious truth, then many citizens not only in Locke's day but also in ours would be inclined to forgo toleration.

The skeptical claim also proves too little, because even if religious truths are unknowable, it does not follow that the state can impose a policy of toleration on citizens who are deeply committed to furthering their religion by saving souls. Toleration, religious citizens might reasonably argue, is no truer—its truth is no more knowable on the basis of reason alone—than their own religious beliefs. Religious citizens whose beliefs rest entirely on faith face similar problems in using the skeptical premise. If they try to justify toleration on the ground that their beliefs, though true, cannot be proved by reason, they in effect grant reason more authority than they do faith, in all of public life. This concession not only reduces the range of activities in which religious claims can be made, but also casts doubt on the authority of religious claims in their own realm. If the need to satisfy the standards of reason is so important as to override faith in so many areas of life, why should one not defer to those standards rather than faith in determining one's own religious beliefs? Alternatively, if faith is so irresistible in determining one's own beliefs, then toleration (which *ex hypothesi*

67

rests only on skepticism) does not seem to have enough weight to override the claims of faith.

Instead of the skeptical premise, the Lockean argument introduces what might be called a validity premise. Although citizens reasonably disagree about matters of religion, and although there may be no way at any particular time to persuade even reasonable people to follow the true religion, it may be the case that there is a true or valid religion, knowable on the basis of, or at least consistent with, reason.[4] Any policy of toleration not only must be consistent with this possibility but also should positively encourage the discovery and promotion of true religious belief.

Notice that this premise, while presupposing the possibility of religious or moral truth, is not so stringent as some more recently proposed criteria that otherwise share the same presupposition. In an important article on moral conflict in politics, Thomas Nagel suggests that to justify state action we must satisfy a higher (ethically based) standard of objectivity: the reasons for the policy must be adjudged true from "a standpoint that is independent of who we are."[5] Nagel's standard seems to exclude too much, however—not only the fundamentalist's belief that God sanctions racial discrimination but also the liberal's belief in human equality (which underlies those coercive state policies that Nagel rightly wants to defend). It would also preclude the conflict over whether the fetus is a person (without which there would be no meaningful public debate over the legalization of abortion). None of these beliefs seems to be justifiable from a standpoint independent of who we are ("a common, objective method of reasoning").[6] Yet they are not equally acceptable (or unacceptable) starting points for public deliberation.

The Lockean argument rejects the neutrality premise in the modern argument for toleration—again for good reason. The purpose of toleration is not to provide equal opportunity for every religious group to flourish, or to make it equally likely that every religion will attract the same number of adherents or increase its congregation at the same rate. This seems impossible, since some religions depend more than others on state support for fulfilling their purposes. Nor does neutrality or impartiality as a moral standard at the level of justification hold any appeal if we can all come to embrace the true religion. If we know what the true religion is, and if the only justification for a governmental policy requires an appeal to religious principles, there is no moral reason to insist on a neutral rationale. If we could be sure that the state would promote the true religion, then we should not want the state to remain neutral or impartial between truth and falsehood, in either its actions or its justifications for actions. But as a matter of historical and political fact, we have good reason not to trust the state to promote the true religion.[7] Instead of neutrality, the Lockean argument appeals to the distrust of government as its basis for defending the second step of the argument. The state should not be permitted to favor one religion over another, because it is at least as likely to favor the false as the true religion.

Finally, although Locke might sympathize with the presumption to defend state inaction on religion, the Lockean argument does not invoke that presumption. In this respect, the argument is more modern than more recent liberal arguments that do rely on the presumption. It should perhaps be even clearer in our time than in Locke's that the failure of the state to act can subject citizens to as much coercion and violation of their rights as a decision to act. Neither action nor inaction by the state should have a privileged status in moral justification. In place of the inaction premise, the Lockean argument introduces a substantive view about the nature of religious belief. The state must not try to command faith by the force of its laws, because true faith cannot by its very nature be commanded. True faith follows rational persuasion.[8] (The secular analogue, which we develop below, holds that democratically formed, collective moral judgments by society must be a matter of deliberation: citizens should choose, deliberately, the principles of public morality.) In place of the premise of inaction, the Lockean argument offers a premise of rational deliberation.

Some religions, of course, do not accept the view that true faith follows rational persuasion, and the Lockean premise will not satisfy their adherents. Were the rationale of religious toleration neutrality, we should criticize such a state policy for not being neutral between citizens who believe that faith can be coerced and those who do not. But the Lockean argument does not claim neutrality among all religions. It is meant to be impartial only among those religions that accept the voluntary nature of faith. For those whose religions are (or can be understood as being) consistent with the claim that religious belief should not be coerced, the argument offers a religious reason for excluding religion from politics. For those whose religion actually requires state coercion, the argument offers only a political reason for excluding religion from politics—the distrust of the state. On the Lockean argument, then, principles of exclusion rest on different grounds for different citizens. The principles are also historically contingent, in that they are more likely to be acceptable in a society in which only a minority practices religions that by their nature require the assistance of state coercion.

Understood in this way, the Lockean premises offer a more plausible (if less general) justification for keeping religious issues off the political agenda than do arguments based on skepticism and neutrality. Can they also serve as a general justification for principles of preclusion? We believe so, but if so the principles thus justified will not preclude as much nonreligious moral conflict as contemporary liberals claim to exclude by the more familiar argument for religious toleration. The Lockean premises will exclude some issues that liberals wish to exclude but admit many others. An example of each will show why.

A policy favoring racial discrimination, it is now generally agreed, deserves no place on the political agenda. Such a policy is not an option that legislatures or citizens should seriously consider, and if they were to do so, we would expect courts to prevent its adoption. Why should racial discrimination be banished from the political agenda and nondiscrimination established as a matter of constitutional right? There are many good reasons for rejecting racial discrimination as a policy or practice, but the argument for completely precluding its consideration for purposes of policy-making must be of a different, stronger kind. Skeptical or neutralist arguments are not sufficient for this purpose, since they imply that racial discrimination, like religion, is a position about which people

70

reasonably disagree. The problem is especially striking when racial discrimination is combined with religious belief. The skeptical argument implies that since some religions sanction racial discrimination on grounds that cannot be rationally refuted, we should agree to disagree on this matter, leaving citizens free to discriminate or not according to the dictates of their religions.

To preclude racial discrimination from reaching the agenda, we need to show that it fails to satisfy the validity premise in the Lockean argument, suitably extended beyond the case of religious conflict. We need an argument showing that the defense of racial discrimination is not a moral position at all. If it is not, then no one can claim that, like religious belief, it is a position about which reasonable citizens might morally disagree. It will fail to satisfy the equivalent of the validity premise in the Lockean argument; we do not assume that it is a position whose validity anyone should seek to discover or establish in our society.

How might one try to show that a position favoring racial discrimination is not in this respect a moral position at all? Some reasons offered in favor of the policy would be disqualified on their face; those that refer to interests based only on the self-interest of whites fail to accept a moral point of view at all. Other reasons might adopt a more general (and seemingly moral) perspective—for instance, the claim that white supremacy benefits blacks more than would social and political equality. These reasons also fail (in a different way) to qualify as moral reasons. They can usually be shown to be rationalizations because the nonmoral basis on which they rest is so tenuous. The alleged benefits of white supremacy are either undefined or defined so narrowly as to exclude relevant considerations, such as the noneconomic prerequisites for living a dignified human life. Or they appeal to empirical evidence but reject all accepted methods of challenging the evidence.

Other reasons may appeal to nonmoral premises that do not purport to make empirical claims in the usual sense—for example, the claim that God speaking literally through the Bible or the laws of nature forbids the mixing of races. These kinds of appeals may be rejected because their basic premises are implausible (and therefore

71

denied even by many people who accept these authorities): if God speaks literally through the Bible, why does so much of the Bible defy literal reading, even on fundamentalist accounts? But the primary reason why such appeals to authority must be rejected as moral reasons is that they close off any possibility of publicly assessing or interpreting the content of the claims put forward by the authority. Appealing to an authority whose dictates are closed to reasonable interpretation cannot constitute a moral reason. To argue otherwise would place no limit at all on the claims that could be made in the name of morality. An appeal to authority certainly can count as a reason, but only when its dictates are open to interpretation by publicly acceptable reasons or methods of inquiry.

No doubt there are other bases on which to deny moral status to claims in favor of racial discrimination, but these should be enough to indicate the kinds of threshold requirements that we should be seeking to determine whether a position satisfies the Lockean validity premise, whether it counts as a moral position at all, and therefore whether it should be precluded from the political agenda. The example of racial discrimination suggests that at least three kinds of requirements are necessary for a position to count as a moral one.[9]

First, there is the familiar (though still controversial) requirement of the moral point of view: the argument for the position must presuppose a disinterested perspective that could be adopted by any member of a society, whatever his or her other particular circumstances (such as class, race, or sex). Satisfying this requirement distinguishes a moral position from one that is merely prudential or self-regarding.[10] Persons whose positions satisfy this requirement in effect declare that they are prepared to enter into a moral discussion. Second, any premises in the argument that depend on empirical evidence or logical inference should in principle be open to challenge by generally accepted methods of inquiry. This requirement ensures that the claims will be accessible to others in the moral discussion, and helps keep the discussion relatively open. Third, premises for which empirical evidence or logical inference is not appropriate should not be radically implausible. Although it is difficult to specify general standards for plausibility, we can say that radically implausible beliefs typically require the rejection of an extensive set of better established beliefs that are widely shared in the society. Such wholesale rejection would significantly diminish the range of considerations that could be invoked in public moral argument.

Thus the political agenda may include some policies based on moral positions that citizens can decide rationally, and some that they cannot. Insofar as a position depends on claims subject to rational argument, it must be criticizable (the second requirement above), and it may therefore turn out to be morally wrong. Insofar as a position does not depend on claims subject to rational argument, its premises need only be not radically implausible (the third requirement). But it still may be criticizable for being less rationally justifiable than competing positions, and policies based on it may be rejected (or accepted) for nonmoral reasons.

Reasonable people, of course, can disagree about what should count as a moral position, but this kind of disagreement seems more susceptible to rational resolution, if only because it abstracts from the reasons and passions that inhere in particular moral conflicts. The abstraction should not be regarded as neutral or formal: it expresses a substantive view about the nature of morality in political contexts—specifically, how citizens should collectively arrive at moral positions. The preclusion requirements reflect (as do the principles of accommodation we discuss below) an ideal of moral deliberation in a democratic process; they constitute part of the conditions necessary to sustain moral discussion among free and equal citizens.[11] Therefore, even if the preclusion requirements do not resolve any particular moral conflict, they remain valid as the only basis on which we can hope to arrive at reasonable resolutions of substantive moral conflicts in the future.

If a policy as abhorrent as racial discrimination can be precluded from reaching the agenda only in something like the way we suggest, then many other moral conflicts that many liberals would like to set aside will stubbornly resist banishment. Abortion is the paradigm of such a dispute, and unlike the parties to a conflict about racial discrimination both sides of the abortion dispute appear to satisfy the threshold requirements for a moral position. Both sides argue from different plausible premises to fundamentally conflicting public policies. Pro-life advocates believe the fetus to be a human being, a person in the generic sense of the term. Their principled basis of opposing legalized abortion is the right of an innocent human to live. Pro-choice advocates believe the fetus to be only a potential person. Their principled basis for championing legalized abortion is a woman's freedom of choice with regard to her own body. Both sides can agree on the general (incompletely specified) moral principles that innocent people have a right to live and that women have a right to freedom of choice with regard to their own bodies. But they arrive at radically different conclusions about abortion because they cannot agree on whether the fetus is a full-fledged person, whether the right to life extends to the obligation of women to realize the human potential of a dependent fetus, and whether women have freedom of choice with regard to their bodies even if the life of an innocent person is at stake.

Insofar as evidence is relevant to the dispute, both sides make claims that are susceptible to accepted methods of inquiry. The pro-life advocate appeals to established scientific facts about the gradual development of a fertilized egg into a viable fetus with the biological characteristics of a human infant, and the pro-choice advocate invokes testable claims about the effects of pregnancy and childbearing on women. Insofar as the premises are based on other kinds of claims (such as whether a fetus is a human being), the premises of neither side are radically implausible or incompatible with the possibility of publicly assessing the content of the claims.

Roger Wertheimer has convincingly argued that pro-choice and pro-life advocates can agree on all the facts about fetuses (and the circumstances of women who bear them) and still disagree in their beliefs about whether the fetus is a person. Different plausible beliefs lie at the base of the best arguments for and against the legalization of abortion.[12] Although pro-life advocates sometimes invoke a religious conception of human life, the belief that the fetus is a human life does not depend on a religious conception. The pro-life

74

belief derives its plausibility from such secular considerations as the similarity of successive stages of fetal development, just as the pro-choice belief partly derives its plausibility from the apparent differences between a zygote and an infant.[13] Both pro-life and pro-choice positions are in this sense reasonable. But reason itself does not "point in either direction: it is *we* who must point it, and *we* who are led by it. If you are led in one direction rather than the other, that is not because of logic, but because you respond in a certain way to certain facts [about the fetus]."[14]

Abortion thus satisfies the requirements of a genuine moral disagreement: the strongest cases both for and against abortion satisfy the three threshold requirements for a moral position. Abortion therefore cannot be precluded from reaching the political agenda on the basis of the generalized version of the first Lockean premise of validity.

It might be supposed that a generalized version of the premise of governmental inaction (part of the modern argument for preclusion) will work for abortion even though it does not work for religion. Wertheimer in effect appeals to such a premise: the government cannot rebut the presumption against inaction in the case of abortion, and therefore should not make it illegal. His argument essentially has three steps: (1) governments cannot restrict freedom unless they can justify their restrictions rationally; (2) neither of the two positions in the debate is more rationally justifiable than the other; and (3) therefore, the government cannot legitimately restrict the freedom of women to have an abortion.[15]

But the argument does not work here any better than it did in the case of religious toleration. By the same form of reasoning that Wertheimer uses to conclude that the government should not act, one could reach the opposite conclusion. From the perspective of those who perceive the fetus as a person, legalization ends the life of the fetus and therefore restricts its freedom absolutely. Without accepting one of the competing views of the fetus, we cannot assume that this restriction on freedom is any more or less justified than a restriction on the freedom of women. Furthermore, we do not in general assume a presumption against the use of governmental coercion if human life is arguably at stake. The premise of the argument for governmental inaction is therefore no more conclusive in the case of abortion than it was in the case of religious conflict.

We have argued that both sides in the abortion controversy satisfy the conditions for a moral position, and that therefore abortion fails the first Lockean premise favoring exclusion from the political agenda. But do either of the two other Lockean premises help preclude the abortion controversy? The second premise—distrust of the government—does not provide the basis for exclusion if there is good reason to trust the government as much as other agents with respect to a given issue. Both sides of the abortion controversy already (reasonably) agree that the government must be trusted with the task of prohibiting murder; there is no more trustworthy agent that can effectively carry out this task. The central question is then whether the government should or should not consider abortion to be murder. Distrusting the government to answer *this* question correctly does not favor one side or the other in the abortion controversy (unless one adds the presumption in favor of inaction, which we have already rejected).

The third Lockean premise favors rational deliberation. Rather than precluding the abortion controversy, it would seem to imply that it should be a subject for collective moral discussion and decision. In the absence of other reasons for preclusion (such as there were in the cases of religion and racial discrimination), this premise suggests that the issue falls within the scope of public policy, even if we collectively decide that abortion should be left to individual moral choice.

The principles of preclusion we have sketched provide an adequate (if underdeveloped) basis for determining whether moral conflict should reach the political agenda. The abortion controversy is the paradigm of a moral conflict that should not be precluded, although modern liberal theory would preclude it. Racial discrimination is the paradigm of a moral conflict that should be precluded, although for reasons different from those offered by modern liberal theory.

Other controversies resemble one of the two paradigms to varying degrees. Capital punishment resembles abortion in that each side at its best seems to hold a position that merits respect. Each can offer reasons for its position that satisfy the threshold conditions of a moral position. Both argue from a disinterested perspective, a concern for preventing unnecessary death, but they give different weights to the risks involved (executing the innocent and protecting victims), and the premises underlying their different weightings are plausible, though their disagreement may not be ultimately resolvable by either moral argument or empirical evidence.

Laws against homosexuality and other policies that discriminate on the basis of sexual orientation resemble the case of racial discrimination. The basis for such policies fails the test of a moral position. Proponents of such policies sometimes adopt a disinterested point of view. But the common claims that homosexual sex causes various kinds of harms have not been supported with solid empirical evidence. Insofar as the case for these discriminatory policies rests on some perception of homosexual sex as unnatural, the position violates the third requirement of a moral position. Nor has a logically consistent argument been constructed on plausible premises to show that homosexual sex cannot be understood as part of the human condition. This is not to deny that many people regard opposition to homosexual sex as part of a sexual morality; it is only to point out that their opposition cannot be supported with the kinds of reasons required for a moral position.

These examples are meant to be merely suggestive. The task of elaborating the principles of preclusion is complex, requiring detailed consideration of subtle features of the moral positions and at the same time considerable refinement of the principles themselves. But the principles we have sketched and the paradigmatic examples of abortion and racial discrimination should be sufficient to suggest the possibility of moving beyond the conventional approaches of neutrality and toleration.

More generally, it is becoming less plausible to deal with all fundamental moral conflict by taking the disputes off the political agenda and leaving the decisions to each individual. Many questions that were once regarded as purely a matter for individuals to decide in private have inescapably become questions of public significance.

77

Political theories that cope with irreconcilable disagreement by a (hypothetical) social agreement to disagree on these questions—letting each individual decide—seem increasingly evasive. They offer a false impartiality in place of social recognition of the persistence of fundamental conflicts of value in our society.

Although it would be worthwhile to develop the principles of preclusion more fully, their role, if our argument so far is correct, is less significant than most liberals have assumed. If we are right that more moral conflict should reach the agenda and become the legitimate subject of legislation, then the critical problems concern the processes by which citizens conduct moral deliberation and the moral reasons they should give in choosing among the substantive policies on the agenda.

Another reason these processes are so important is that it is through collective moral deliberation over time that citizens can (and should) decide which particular positions come to deserve a place on the political agenda. The preclusion principles are sensitive to changes in social and political attitudes. Perhaps citizens one hundred years ago should have regarded discrimination against homosexuals as failing to meet the standards of a moral position at all, but citizens today have stronger grounds for taking this view. Because of the nature of social practices and the relative lack of public debate about the subject, many citizens at an earlier time may not have had an adequate opportunity to explore the full implications of their arguments.

Furthermore, those who morally opposed discrimination could not themselves be so confident of their position, until they had tested their moral views over time in various circumstances and subjected them to the experience and evidence that is now more widely available. They come to see that, after ample opportunity for argument, the defenders of discrimination offer little more than expressions of personal preference. Even if there is nothing inherent in a moral view itself that renders it beyond the pale of moral discourse, it may be disqualified, as discrimination against homosexuals is coming to be disqualified, by our common recognition of the moral vacuity of the case for it.

Principles of Accommodation

In seeking principles for political consensus in the face of fundamental moral disagreement, we need to attend not only to the nature of the positions but also to the way in which people hold or express positions. Morally respectable positions can be defended in morally disrespectful ways. It is the role of the principles of accommodation to restrain those ways. These principles govern the relations among citizens who hold morally legitimate though fundamentally opposed positions on public policy. They suggest how citizens who disagree about an issue should treat each other with regard to that issue and related issues, even when the policy debate results in legislation and the state takes a position favoring one side of the dispute. The principles are best conceived as expressing a virtue that lies at the core of moral deliberation in a democracy—mutual respect.

Like toleration, mutual respect is a form of agreeing to disagree. But mutual respect demands more than toleration. It requires a favorable attitude toward, and constructive interaction with, the persons with whom one disagrees. It consists in a reciprocal positive regard of citizens who manifest the excellence of character that permits a democracy to flourish in the face of (at least temporarily) irresolvable moral conflict.[16]

Mutual respect manifests a distinctively democratic kind of character—the character of individuals who are morally committed, self-reflective about their commitments, discerning of the difference between respectable and merely tolerable differences of opinion, and open to the possibility of changing their minds or modifying their positions at some time in the future if they confront unanswerable objections to their present point of view. The significance of this kind of character, and the justification for giving it a privileged place in dealing with moral conflict in a democracy, can finally be established only through a detailed interpretation of its specific virtues in a political context.[17] We present the outline of such an interpretation below, but two general considerations that tell in its favor can be mentioned.

First, mutual respect seems to be necessary to keep open the possibility of resolving, on a moral basis, any significant dispute about public policy that involves fundamental moral conflict. If citizens do not practice mutual respect as they try to come to agreement on a morally disputed policy, or as they try to live with the disagreement that remains after the disputed policy is adopted, they are forced to turn to nonmoral ways of dealing with moral conflict. They are driven to count on procedural agreements, political deals, and threats of violence—all of which obviously stand in the way of moral deliberation. The underlying assumption is that we should value reaching conclusions through reason rather than force, and more specifically through moral reasoning rather than through self-interested bargaining. Citizens and officials, we assume, can learn how to take each other seriously as moral agents. They can enter the discussion in the political forum with the purpose of discovering principles on which the society as a whole can act, rather than with the aim of devising arguments by which they can advance only their own interests.

The presumption in favor of reason is itself contestable, but it should not be contested on grounds that it grants a higher value to political procedures than to moral substance of outcomes. Mutual respect makes possible, at the level of political decision, the deliberate choice of substantive moral values for the society as a whole. It is the moral value of choosing moral values, then, that (partly) justifies the prominence of moral reasoning in the political process. (In this respect, its justification recalls the Lockean premise that presumes that faith cannot be commanded.)

Second, mutual respect can contribute not only to social good but also to individual virtue. Persons who practice mutual respect are disposed against the premature moral skepticism, and the concomitant ennui and indecision that afflict those who treat the existence of conflicting opinions as proof of the arbitrariness of all moral judgments. ("You have your opinion and I have mine, and who's to say who's right?") They are also less inclined toward moral dogmatism, and its accompanying anger and arrogance, which is common among those who treat moral disagreement as a sure sign of the ignorance or depravity of their opponents. ("Either you're for killing babies or you're against killing babies," declared Nellie Gray, the leader of a March for Life in Washington.[18] "Either you're for the liberation of women or you're against it" is the analogous dogmatism of some pro-choice advocates.)

Being reciprocal, mutual respect makes two general kinds of demands of persons: the first specifies how one presents one's own moral position; the second, how one regards others' moral positions. The principles of accommodation, which spell out these demands, thus require that citizens affirm the moral status of their own position and acknowledge the moral status of their opponents' position.

Although the principles refer to the way that opinions are held and expressed, their object is not mainly a matter of style or rhetoric but, rather, of attitude and conduct as manifested in public actions. What they seek is not only speech but also action, and not only action but also action in cooperation with others over time. Their object is a family of dispositions, which constitutes an excellence of public character that we expect democratic citizens to exhibit.

The first set of principles—calling on citizens to affirm the moral status of their own positions—involves a kind of moral or characterological integrity. There are no doubt many ways that citizens could demonstrate such integrity, but at least three seem important in politics. First, we expect citizens and officials to espouse their moral positions independently of the circumstances in which they speak. This is consistency in speech and is a sign of political sincerity: it indicates that a person holds the position because it is a moral position, not for reasons of political advantage. There is of course no completely reliable way to tell if such a principle is satisfied. It is difficult enough in private life to judge sincerity; in the more distant relations of public life, sincerity becomes so hard to confirm that we (perhaps too easily) assume that hypocrisy is all there is. But we should be able to find more reliable criteria for recognizing, or at least providing good grounds for suspecting, insincerity. Politicians who continually shift their positions according to political advantage give us good grounds for doubting that they honestly accept on moral grounds any of the positions they espouse.

81

We should not think much of the moral seriousness of someone who expressed a moral position, however consistently, but never acted on it. We therefore need a second principle that requires one to act in ways consistent with the positions one holds. This is the most familiar form of integrity—consistency between speech and action. The pro-choice advocate who prevents a daughter from having an abortion over her strong objection, the staunch opponent of legalized abortion who helps a daughter obtain an abortion—both fall short of acting in ways that warrant the respect of their fellow citizens. Failing to act may also be culpable. We legitimately expect people who accept positions of public responsibility to act according to their professed beliefs unless constrained by some overriding duty of office. Disrespect is due politicians who in a campaign emphasize their concern over abortion but, once elected to office, fail (out of laziness or lack of leadership) to work for the policies implied by the position they advocated.

Finally, we might reasonably question the moral seriousness of someone who, though speaking and acting consistently on a particular position, refuses to recognize and act on its consequences for other, related issues. Hence the need for a third principle: citizens should accept the broader implications of the principles presupposed by their moral positions. This is integrity of principle. Those who oppose abortion out of respect for fetal life should be equally strong advocates of policies to ensure that children are properly fed. Sometimes there may be good reasons for denying the apparent implications (perhaps because other, more weighty moral considerations may block the natural inference). But if so, the burden should be on those who would deny the implications. A pro-life advocate who opposes the program of Aid to Families of Dependent Children on grounds, for example, that it is inefficient and mismanaged should also seek alternative public policies that would go at least as far in protecting the health and welfare of poor children.

The second set of principles of accommodation, which calls on citizens to acknowledge the moral status of the positions they oppose, also seeks to develop aspects of democratic character. They parallel the three principles prescribing forms of integrity, but since they look outward toward one's judgments of others, they may be thought of as forms of magnanimity.

First, acknowledging the moral status of a position that one opposes requires, at a minimum, that one treat it as a moral rather than a purely political, economic, or other kind of nonmoral view. This acknowledgment in speech begins with the recognition that an opponent's position is based on moral principles about which reasonable people may disagree (provided that it meets the preclusion conditions for reaching the political agenda). An illustration of this kind of acknowledgment is the appeal in the House by a Congressman opposing a motion that would deny government funding for abortions in the case of rape or incest:

> Let me at the outset say that I understand the depth of feeling of those who support the motion, and who feel that abortion should be permitted only when the life of the mother is in danger. I understand the sincerity with which those who advocate that position come to the floor. . . . Now, I know that obviously [our] position [in favor of funding abortions in cases of rape or incest] is one that is morally inconsistent with the position of those who are supporting the motion, but I suggest to you that it is certainly an understandable, defensible position, and one which I would hope those who do not like abortion would nonetheless understand . . . I would hope that they would at least acknowledge that there is . . . moral controversy.[19]

In the debate that followed, many members, in the tone and content of their arguments, did in fact acknowledge the moral nature of the controversy.[20]

This debate stands in contrast with an earlier one in the House, also on abortion funding, in which members manifested less respect for the moral seriousness of their opponents. At one point in that debate, a Congressman argued against abortion funding on the grounds that it would increase the federal deficit. "If we are going to pay off this debt, somebody has got to be born to pay the taxes to pay it off."[21] This prompted the next speaker to throw away her prepared remarks, and attack him for ignoring the moral issue: "We are talking about matters of life."[22]

There are of course many other ways of denying the moral status of an opponent's position—perhaps the most rampant is claiming that a position is politically motivated—but what they all seem to have in common is the refusal to give moral reasons for rejecting the position. We show respect for persons by joining with them in serious and sustained moral discussion on the issue in question and on other issues that divide us. In such discussion, we not only state publicly our reasons for rejecting opponents' positions but also invite and consider carefully responses to our objections.

Mutual acknowledgment in this kind of moral discussion could drift toward a merely formal, ritualistic expression of mutual respect, unless there is some real possibility that each side may be moved by the reasons the other gives. Therefore, a second principle (paralleling the requirement of integrity in action) is needed to keep open the possibility that citizens could come to adopt and act on the position of their opponents. It requires citizens to cultivate a disposition toward openness. We should try to break personal and institutional habits that discourage the chance that we might accept the position of our opponents at some time in the future, or at least modify our own position in the direction of that of our opponents. Both the political mind and the political forum should be kept open to reconsideration of decisions already made and policies already adopted.

The disposition toward openness does not imply that political change is good in itself, or even that an open mind is the most virtuous form of character. It is, or should be, compatible with affirming one's own moral views strongly and consistently. We should be seeking a balance between holding firm convictions and being prepared to change them if we encounter objections that on reflection we cannot answer. Maintaining this delicate balance is no doubt psychologically (as well as intellectually) demanding, but the personal and political dangers of a psychologically simpler path, succumbing to moral dogmatism on the one hand or moral skepticism on the other, are greater.[23]

Although the disposition toward openness is elusive, especially in politics, we can sometimes detect its absence or presence even in the statements of public officials. Consider the difference in emphasis in statements by Joseph Califano and Mario Cuomo on the question of abortion. Writing about his struggle with the abortion issue during his tenure as Secretary of Health, Education, and Welfare, Califano commented, "I concluded that it was not sufficient simply to express my view clearly and consistently, but that it was also essential to communicate *the certainty with which I held it*. Any hedging would only encourage those who disagreed, to hope for a change that would not be forthcoming."[24] In a nationally publicized speech at Notre Dame University, Governor Mario Cuomo defended his position on the legalization of abortion this way: "I [am] eager for enlightenment, eager to learn new and better ways to manifest respect for the deep reverence for life that is our religion and our instinct. I hope that the public attempt to describe the problems as I understand them, will give impetus to the dialogue in the Catholic community and beyond, a dialogue which could show me a better wisdom than I've been able to find so far."[25]

Because the contexts differ, we cannot be sure that the statements actually show a difference in the views or dispositions of the two speakers, but on its face Cuomo's speech shows a greater commitment to openness than does Califano's comment. Cuomo seems more inclined to consider the possibility of changing his mind on the abortion question. At the least, his speech invites further discussion and calls for continuing the dialogue on the issue. It holds open the possibility of moral change and thus manifests moral regard for the position that it opposes.

Cuomo's speech is characterized not only by openness but also by a commitment to seek a common perspective at a deeper level of morality ("reverence for life") that could transcend moral differences at the level of policy. This is an instance of a third form of magnanimity, another way of acknowledging the moral status of others' positions: in justifying policies on moral grounds, we should seek the rationale that minimizes rejection of the position we oppose.[26] While the corresponding (and compatible) requirement of integrity calls on us to accept the broader implications of our positions, this principle of magnanimity tells us to avoid unnecessary

85

conflict in characterizing the moral grounds or drawing out the policy implications of our positions. The principle encourages what we may call an economy of moral disagreement at both foundational and policy levels of political argument.[27] It does not ask us to compromise our moral understandings in the interest of agreement but rather to search for significant points of convergence between our own understandings and those of citizens whose positions, taken in their more comprehensive forms, we must reject.

Some of the best work in practical moral philosophy can be interpreted as seeking such an economy. In one of the most widely cited philosophical analyses of abortion, Judith Jarvis Thomson succeeds in narrowing the range of disagreement between pro-life and pro-choice advocates to cases where pregnancy is largely voluntary.[28] By means of several hypothetical examples, she shows that even people who perceive the fetus to be a person should acknowledge that abortion may be justified in circumstances where pregnancy is the result of forced intercourse. That is part of the point of her well-known example of the unconscious violinist with kidney failure, who has been plugged into your circulatory system against your will. The violinist's survival depends on his remaining plugged into you for nine months, but he does not have a right to remain attached to you if you object.[29] The example is meant to suggest that it may sometimes be morally permissible (though not admirable) to kill an innocent person even if your own life is not at stake. The example should convince even people who perceive the fetus to be a full-fledged person that it is not obviously unjust for women who become pregnant through no fault of their own (e.g., by rape or incest) to be legally free to obtain abortions.

The political distance remaining between pro-life and pro-choice advocates is, of course, still great. In the vast majority of cases in which women seek abortions, where pregnancy is not the result of force, Thomson's arguments leave pro-choice and pro-life advocates radically opposed. Even in this treacherous territory of rationally irresolvable disagreement, there is still some prospect for further accommodation. For example, the grounds on which governments decide the questions should comply with the economy of moral disagreement.

If the government decides to permit (or even fund) abortion, it should be on grounds that acknowledge as far as possible the moral legitimacy of the pro-life position.

To some extent, the Supreme Court in *Roe v. Wade* did just that. Although the Court did not admit as a constitutional argument the claim that fetuses are persons, the majority opinion emphasized that the state has an interest in protecting the potential of life.[30] This emphasis moved the rationale for the decision closer to the conclusions of a pro-life position, particularly in the later stages of fetal development, and did so without abandoning the premise that fetuses are not persons. The Court, with consistency, allowed states to ban abortion in the third trimester, on the grounds that the state's interest in potential life is compelling once the fetus is viable. If medical technology advances and viability extends to earlier stages of pregnancy, then the Court's rationale, on this logic, should give increasing protection to fetal life. Otherwise, states are required to protect a woman's right to an abortion.

Because the Court did not let this logic prevail, it did not move as far as it might have in the direction of mutual respect. In its discussion of the second trimester of pregnancy, the Court introduced a consideration that is required by neither pro-life nor pro-choice premises: the claim that the state has a compelling interest in protecting the health of pregnant women even against their own will.[31] The Court's only rationale for this claim was that second-trimester abortions are riskier than normal childbirth. Yet the Court has not consistently followed the implications of its own rationale: it has been unwilling to judge restrictions on second-trimester abortions according to whether they are necessary to equalize the risks of abortion and normal childbirth. Moreover, having granted the state's interest in protecting potential life, the Court failed to offer a credible moral (or constitutional) argument for giving priority to the state's interest in protecting maternal health over its interest in protecting potential life. Protecting maternal health may be reasonable grounds for restricting abortions, but the Court failed to offer good reasons for giving it priority over protecting potential life.

Not only is the Court's justification of the second-trimester criterion incompletely argued and inconsistently applied but it also ignores a crucial question: if viability extends into earlier phases of fetal development, should states be permitted to regulate abortions in the second trimester as well as in the third? Although we are not sure what the court would have said had it actually tried to answer this question, the implicit answer seems to be that paternalistic protection of consenting adults deserves more constitutional weight than protection of potential life, even when that life is imminently actual. The absence of an explicit answer in *Roe v. Wade* has come back to haunt the Court in its recent *Webster* decision. The opinion in *Webster* reveals not only disagreement but also confusion over the rationale of the trimester criterion in *Roe v. Wade*.[32]

Rejecting any rationale based on the value of prenatal life, and relying instead on a paternalistic rationale for regulating second-trimester abortions, the Court in effect invited states to invent dubious medical rationales referring to maternal health in order to defend laws that were actually intended to protect prenatal life.[33] In failing to follow its own rationale (which implies equalizing the risks of abortion and natural childbirth), the Court left itself without a principled way of distinguishing between paternalistic restrictions intended to protect maternal health (limiting the freedom of women for their own good) and those intended to protect prenatal life. The Court's reliance on this paternalistic rationale for restricting second-trimester abortions has thereby rendered its judgment more divisive and less open to change through rational deliberation than a public philosophy would prescribe.

Not only judges and legislators but also citizens should be expected to practice the economy of moral disagreement. They ought to be able to agree, for example, that someone's views on abortion should not affect how she is treated in other respects. A pro-lifer ought not to favor denying a woman who has an abortion access to other essential medical care. A pro-choicer ought not to refuse pro-lifers the right to speak against abortion even in front of an abortion clinic.

Officials and citizens can also minimize the areas of their public disagreement by promoting policies on which their principles converge, even if they would otherwise place those policies significantly lower on their own list of political priorities. Although pro-choice advocates may think publicly funded programs that help unwed mothers care for their own children are less important than pro-life proponents do, pro-choice advocates should join in actively promoting these programs and other policies that are similarly consistent with the principles of both sides. By trying to maximize political agreement in these ways, we do not end serious moral conflict, but we affirm that we accept significant parts of the substantive morality of fellow citizens to whom we may find ourselves deeply opposed in other respects.

The politics of mutual respect is not always pretty. The deliberation that takes place among citizens and public officials under the principles of accommodation may be quite robust. Citizens may find it necessary to make extreme and uncompromising statements and to refuse to cooperate with opponents. These strategies may be justified when, for example, they are necessary to gain attention for a legitimate position that would otherwise be ignored, and therefore to promote mutual respect in the long run. Even if it does not promise a comprehensive common good, a philosophy of mutual respect does seek agreement on substantive moral values for the society. By thus raising the moral stakes of politics, it may, at least in the short run, increase moral conflict in politics.

Mutual respect, as expressed through the principles of accommodation, thus requires an effort to appreciate the moral force of the positions of people with whom we disagree. But at least as important as these individual efforts are the demands on political institutions. To fulfill those demands, we may need to consider changes in our institutions, and perhaps the creation of new ones. The principles of accommodation (or, for that matter, the principles of preclusion) do not justify social or legal prohibitions on what citizens may say in the public forum; in this respect, they are meant to be consistent with conventional liberal doctrines of free speech. But the principles of accommodation not only permit, but may require, changing the balance of institutional influences on public deliberation.

The principles imply that the forums in which we conduct our political discussion should be designed so as to encourage officials to justify their actions with moral reasons and to give other officials as well as citizens the opportunity to criticize those reasons. Legislators, for example, might act more like judges by assuming a regular responsibility to explain in writing, in principled terms, the basis for their decisions. To encourage the virtue of openness, we could ensure that our institutions permit reconsideration of important moral decisions and policies at regular intervals. Although unlimited opportunities to reopen questions would of course paralyze government, some of the existing barriers to fundamental changes may be too high. The procedures for amending the constitution, for example, make the possibility of future change in some major policies seem hopelessly remote. To promote an economy of moral disagreement, we might fashion more broad-based political organizations that permit citizens who hold different moral positions to work together on other causes whose goals they share. In this respect, a fluid and open party system would be more desirable than a political structure dominated by single-issue groups.

The merits of these particular institutional suggestions would have to be considered in the context of many different political factors, and other changes may turn out to be more constructive.[34] The point of the suggestions is to emphasize that the principles of accommodation not only impose duties on individuals but also carry implications for institutions. Mutual respect is a political virtue, and as such it is shaped by the institutions in which it is practiced.

A Public Philosophy

Practicing the virtue of mutual respect as we propose here would create a broader kind of political consensus and thus expand the scope of what may be called the public philosophy—those sets of moral principles on which reasonable citizens should agree, whatever moral principles they hold privately. Such a public philosophy would embrace not only principles that protect basic rights (such as nondiscrimination) and principles that justify certain procedures (such as majority rule) but also principles that govern the conduct of moral relations in public life.

This kind of public philosophy would avoid the dichotomy that has come to dominate contemporary discussions of political theory, which poses a choice between basing politics on a comprehensive conception of the good, on the one hand, or limiting politics to a conception of procedural justice, on the other. We can and should avoid choosing either of these approaches exclusively. The quest for agreement on a conception of the good (the aim, for example, of some communitarian theories)[35] underestimates the significance and legitimate persistence of fundamental moral disagreement. In a pluralist society, comprehensive moral theories neither can nor should win the agreement of all citizens. A public philosophy for such societies must reject the unqualified quest for agreement because it must renounce the claim to comprehensiveness. This is part of the point of interpreting the principles of preclusion in the way that we do: we recognize that the political agenda will never be free of fundamental moral disagreement. Deliberating about the substantive moral values underlying policy does not guarantee that citizens will agree on a coherent set of those values, or on many values at all.

The rejection of comprehensiveness as an aim, as we have argued, does not imply skepticism, whether moral or metaphysical. On the contrary, it reflects the core commitment to a conception of politics that is conducive to moral deliberation and to a conception of persons whose convictions are guided by their moral deliberations. Like the Lockean premise that posits that religious belief should not be commanded, the foundation of mutual respect presupposes that moral choices, and in particular collective moral choices, should be made deliberately. In opening forums of political decision-making to a wide range of legitimate moral disagreement, and defending the practices within those forums that cultivate mutual regard among citizens, mutual respect supports a political process that promotes moral learning. Citizens put their moral beliefs to the test

91

of public deliberation and strengthen their convictions or change their minds in response to the arguments in which they engage, under conditions governed by the principles of accommodation.

This process goes beyond the proceduralism that many liberals favor. Unlike theories that would minimize the moral content of politics, a public philosophy of mutual respect accepts the need to promote substantive moral principles in politics—principles that could become part of a public morality for the society as a whole. Although the policy prescriptions of mutual respect may be less comprehensive, the prescriptions for political deliberation are more comprehensive—and more demanding—than those of other moral doctrines. In cultivating the virtue of open-minded commitment among citizens, and in encouraging an economy of moral disagreement in politics, mutual respect orients the deliberations of citizens and public officials toward a view of the common good—a common good that is compatible with continuing moral disagreement. This common good is constituted partly by those substantive rights and obligations on which many moral philosophies converge and partly by a public search for additional moral agreement.

A public philosophy of the kind we are urging aims at both less and more than the "overlapping consensus" that John Rawls describes as the political foundation for justice.[36] A public philosophy aims at less than Rawls's theory by permitting, under certain conditions, disagreement on aspects of the basic structure itself. Political agreement may be undesirable even when the basic structure of a society is at issue (as it is in the abortion controversy, in which the question of who should count as a member of society is in dispute). In deference to the demands of mutual respect, the policy prescriptions of a public philosophy are in this respect less comprehensive than those of most moral doctrines, including Rawls's. Mutual respect does not guarantee that all public policies produced by the process it governs will fit the conventional liberal program.

But mutual respect also aims at more than Rawlsian justice because it continues to seek agreement on substantive moral principles—even comprehensive ones—that could guide citizens and public officials acting within the basic structure. Rawls "removes from the political agenda the most divisive issues, pervasive uncertainty and serious contention about which must undermine the bases of social cooperation."[37] He leaves citizens to dispute in public primarily those moral views that potentially unite them.[38] In an argument with non-Catholics about nuclear deterrence, Catholics could appeal to their own theology, but only insofar as they rely on principles that can be presented as consistent with the fundamental principles of their opponents. "We do not state more of our comprehensive view than we think would advance the quest for consensus."[39] Appealing to distinctively Catholic principles would not serve the important goal of achieving an overlapping consensus. Similarly, insofar as the Catholic doctrine on abortion serves politically to divide citizens on this issue, the Rawlsian position counsels political silence (though of course it does not require it). Comprehensive moral theories contribute constructively to politics on his view only to the extent that they serve as a source of common principles.

By contrast, mutual respect requires citizens to strive not only for agreement on principles governing the basic structure but also for agreement on practices governing the way they deal with principled disagreements, whether about the basic structure or about ordinary policies. Agreement on these practices is possible because citizens who seriously disagree over policies such as the legalization of abortion, capital punishment, and pornography can share other substantive standards: they can recognize that their own moral commitments might turn out to be wrong even though they now have good reason to believe them to be true; they can value public deliberation as a critical means of subjecting their moral commitments to critical scrutiny (and possibly changing them in the future); and they can give serious consideration to opposing points of view as a manifestation of their respect for morally reasonable people. Because we should agree on how to be morally governed in our political behavior, even when we morally disagree on fundamental political issues, a public philosophy should be more comprehensive than Rawls suggests.

In the pursuit of principles of mutual respect, we move from seeking agreement on the level of legislation or the basic institutional structure of society to the level of political deliberation. A public philosophy emphasizing mutual respect articulates a consensus on the conditions for political discussion of enduring moral disagreement. This shift in the level on which agreement is sought is significant, both theoretically and practically. Theoretically, this kind of public philosophy expresses as complete a conception of politics as is possible within a morally pluralistic society. It seeks agreement on how publicly to deliberate when citizens fundamentally (and reasonably) disagree, rather than on how to purge politics of disagreement. Practically, a public philosophy reminds citizens of the collective risks they run if they individually continue merely to disagree in politics without also searching for ways to foster respect for the moral differences that give rise to moral conflict. A public philosophy incorporating the principles of preclusion and accommodation that we have suggested would direct practical efforts as much toward methods of dealing with irreconcilable disagreements as toward the means of resolving them.

3

Deliberative Democracy beyond Process

Theories of deliberative democracy incorporate a set of principles that are intended to establish fair terms of political cooperation in a democratic society. Some theorists believe that the principles should inform only the process of making political decisions in government or civil society.[1] The principles of deliberative democracy, they argue, should not prescribe the content of the laws, but only the procedures (such as equal suffrage) by which laws are made and the conditions (such as free political speech) under which the procedures can be made to work fairly. These theorists, whom we call pure proceduralists, insist that democratic theory should not incorporate substantive principles such as individual liberty or equal opportunity beyond what is necessary to ensure a fair democratic process. They do not deny that substantive principles such as freedom of religion, nondiscrimination, or basic health care are important, but they wish to keep these principles out of their democratic theories.

We argue that this effort to keep democratic theory procedurally pure fails, and that any adequate theory must include substantive as well as procedural principles. Our own theory, presented in *Democracy and Disagreement*, offers one such approach: it includes substantive principles (such as basic liberty and fair opportunity) that extend fairness to persons (for the sake of reciprocity, mutual respect, or fairness itself). Principles of basic liberty and fair opportunity can be defended on many substantive grounds; in that book we argue from a widely recognized principle of reciprocity or mutual justification among persons who are bound by the laws of a democracy.

But our argument here does not depend on accepting the book's theory whole, or even the specific grounds of reciprocity on which we base the principles. We wish to maintain here that, on a wide range of available grounds, democratic principles must be substantive as well as procedural. A democratic theory that shuns substantive principles for the sake of remaining purely procedural sacrifices an essential value of democracy itself: its principles cannot claim to treat citizens in the way that free and equal persons should be treated—whether fairly, reciprocally, or with mutual respect—in a democratic society in which laws bind all equally.

Pure proceduralists make two kinds of arguments against including substantive principles—one from moral authority and the other from political authority. The argument from moral authority holds that the moral judgment of democratic citizens, not democratic theorists, should determine the content of laws. A theory that contains substantive principles improperly preempts the moral authority of citizens. The argument from political authority maintains that substantive principles similarly preempt the political sovereignty of citizens, which should be exercised not through hypothetical theoretical reasoning but through actual democratic decision-making. A theory that contains substantive principles unduly constrains the democratic decision-making process, including the process of deliberation itself.

We dispute both of these arguments and defend the inclusion of substantive principles in a theory of deliberative democracy. We agree with those theorists who point out that mere procedures, such as majority rule, cannot justify outcomes that are unjust according to substantive principles. But these same theorists usually neglect the substantive value in the procedures, and often assume that an outcome is fully justified if it satisfies substantive principles that are completely distinct from process.

In any case, our main argument against pure proceduralism is not simply the standard objection that procedures can produce unjust outcomes, though we accept this objection. We also argue for including substantive principles in a democratic theory for another, generally neglected reason. Such principles should be included so that the theory can explicitly recognize that both substantive and procedural principles are subject to contestation in similar ways. A critical claim in our defense of a deliberative democratic theory that is both procedural and substantive is that the principles are to be treated as morally and politically provisional. This provisionality gives deliberation part of its point. Both procedural and substantive principles are systematically open to revision in an ongoing process of moral and political deliberation. If the principles are understood in this way, the usual objections against including substantive principles lose their force. The provisional status of all its principles thus constitutes a distinctive strength of deliberative democratic theory, and at the same time offers deliberative democrats an effective response to those who would exclude substantive principles from democratic theory.

Although we concentrate here on showing the problems inherent in the form of pure proceduralism that justifies political outcomes by procedural criteria only, our general criticisms also apply against any attempt to segregate procedural and substantive principles in separate theories. Theorists who judge outcomes partly by substantive principles of justice are still pure proceduralists (with respect to their democratic theories) if they assume that the democratic procedures can be justified without reference to some of the same substantive values expressed by their principles of justice. Our argument is intended to show that this kind of sharp separation between procedural and substantive principles and theories is not sustainable.

To illustrate some of the major points in the argument for including both procedural and substantive principles in a deliberative democratic theory, we draw upon a case involving deliberation about health care in the United Kingdom. In 1999, the British Government created a new body, the National Institute for Clinical Excellence (NICE), which is to provide assessments of treatments and clinical guidelines for use by the National Health Service (NHS).

The impetus for the new Institute came from the widespread recognition that the NHS could not fund care for all health needs,
and needed to find a way to make its difficult decisions in a more
public and deliberative manner.[2] By creating a deliberative decision-
making body, which includes both expert and lay members, the
British Government may also have hoped that it could defuse some
of the controversy about the hard choices that had to be made.
But not surprisingly, shortly after its creation, NICE itself came
under criticism in another deliberative forum—the House of Commons. Together these moments of deliberation—the proceedings of
NICE and the Commons debate about NICE—are more appropriate for our purposes than cases from the United States. They involve an attempt to institutionalize nationwide deliberation about
health-care priorities in a way that the United States has tried only
in certain states. Also, the deliberation takes place in a nation in
which principles of justice in health care come closer to being satisfied than in the United States, and therefore poses a greater challenge to our claim that such principles are necessary in any adequate
theory of deliberative democracy. If a theory needs substantive principles when applied to health care in the United Kingdom, then a
fortiori it should need them when applied to similar issues in the
United States.

Why Reciprocity Requires Deliberation

To determine what kinds of principles belong in a deliberative democratic theory, we need first to consider the meaning and implications
of the fundamental principle of reciprocity. Reciprocity is widely recognized as a core principle of democracy in its many moral varia-
tions—liberal, constitutional, procedural, and deliberative—but most
theories do not give it the central role that deliberative democracy does. Reciprocity holds that citizens owe one another justifications for the mutually binding laws and public policies they collectively enact. The aim of a theory that takes reciprocity seriously is to
help people seek political agreement on the basis of principles that

can be justified to others who share the aim of reaching such an agreement.

Mutual justification means not merely offering reasons to other people, or even offering reasons that they happen to accept (for example, because they are in a weak bargaining position). It means providing reasons that constitute a justification for imposing binding laws on them. What reasons count as such a justification is inescapably a substantive question. Merely formal standards for mutual justification—such as a requirement that the maxims implied by laws be generalizable—are not sufficient. If the maxim happens to be "maximize self- or group-interest," generalizing it does not ensure that justification is mutual. Something similar could be said about all other conceivable candidates for formal standards. Mutual justification requires reference to substantive values.

We can see more clearly why mutual justification cannot proceed without relying on substantive values by imagining any set of reasons that would deny persons basic opportunities, such as equal suffrage and essential health care. Even if the reasons satisfied formal standards, they could not constitute a mutual justification because those deprived of the basic opportunities could reasonably reject them. Denying some persons suffrage is a procedural deprivation that is inconsistent with reciprocity: we cannot justify coercive laws to persons who had no share in making them. Similarly, denying persons essential health care is a substantive deprivation that cannot be justified to the individuals who need it. That such denials are unacceptable shows that the mutual justification is neither purely formal nor purely procedural.

Because such denials of basic opportunities cannot be mutually justifiable, the principles of a democratic theory must be both procedural and substantive. A democratic theory whose principles would permit some persons to be unnecessarily deprived of a basic opportunity like health care does not take seriously the value of mutual justification implied by the principle of reciprocity. Furthermore, it does not treat persons as free and equal beings. Although we argue from the fundamental principle of reciprocity, this principle converges in its implications with the ideal of free and equal personhood, which is the basis of many democratic theories, not only deliberative ones.

The principles of our deliberative democratic theory specify terms of cooperation that satisfy reciprocity. Such terms are similar to what John Rawls calls "fair terms of social cooperation." But the procedural and substantive content of fair terms of social cooperation will vary with different interpretations of what reciprocity requires. A theory is "deliberative" if the fair terms of social cooperation include the requirement that citizens or their representatives actually seek to give one another mutually acceptable reasons to justify the laws they adopt. The reasons, as we have seen, refer to substantive values no less than to procedural ones.

Although reciprocity is a foundational value in deliberative democracy, it does not play the same role that first principles, such as utility or liberty, play in theories such as utilitarianism or libertarianism. These theories derive all of their other principles from their first principles. Reciprocity is not a first principle from which the rest of justice is derived, but rather a regulatory principle that serves two different roles. First, it guides thinking in the ongoing process in which citizens as well as theorists consider what justice requires in the case of particular laws in specific contexts. Second, it shows the need to fill out the content of a deliberative democratic theory with other principles. Reciprocity points to the need to develop such principles as publicity, accountability, basic liberty, basic opportunity, and fair opportunity, which are necessary for the mutual justification of laws. As the first role of reciprocity suggests, such principles should be developed in an actual ongoing process of mutual justification.

An important implication of reciprocity is that democratic deliberation—the process of mutual reason-giving—is not equivalent to the hypothetical justifications proposed by some social contract theories. Such justifications may constitute part of the moral reasoning to which some citizens appeal, but the reasoning must survive the test of actual deliberation if it is to ground laws that actually bind all citizens. Moreover, deliberation should take place not only in the private homes of citizens or the studies of philosophers but in public political forums. In this respect, deliberative theory proposes a political ideal that is process-dependent, even if its content is not exclusively process-oriented.

The requirement that actual deliberation take place is not simply a matter of trying to ensure that citizens feel that their views were taken into account even when they disagree with the outcome. Actual political deliberation at some time is required to justify the law for this society at this time. The reason-giving process is necessary for declaring a law to be not only legitimate but also just. The process is necessary to give assurance that (substantive or procedural) principles that may be right in general are also right in the particular case or rightly applied to this particular case. No amount of hypothetical reasoning is likely to bring out all the complexities that are relevant to determining whether a law is justified at a particular time in any given society. It would be difficult to decide on the basis of any general principle of basic opportunity whether, for example, NICE was justified in denying coverage for a new anti-flu drug (zanamivir) marketed as Relenza by the pharmaceutical company Glaxo-Wellcome.[3] What would be missing is not simply factual information but the weighing of facts and the balancing of values in the context of other health care and related decisions that officials as well as citizens need to make.

It may be helpful to think of the requirement of actual deliberation as analogous to a feature of scientific inquiry. Reciprocity is to justice in political ethics what replication is to truth in scientific ethics. A finding of truth in science requires replicability, which calls for public demonstration. A finding of justice in political ethics requires reciprocity, which calls for public deliberation. Deliberation is not sufficient to establish justice, but deliberation at some point in history is necessary. Just as repeated replication is unnecessary once the truth of a finding (such as the law of gravity) has been amply confirmed, so repeated deliberation is unnecessary once a precept of justice (such as equal protection under the laws) has been extensively deliberated. (Deliberation may still be desirable, of course, even when justice does not demand it.)

The practice of actual deliberation—giving justifying reasons for mutually binding laws to one's fellow citizens—itself both exemplifies and promotes the value of reciprocity. Citizens who have effective opportunities to deliberate treat one another not merely as objects who are to be judged by theoretical principles but also as subjects who can accept or reject the reasons given for the laws that mutually bind them. The reasons are not to be regarded as binding unless they are presented to citizens who have the chance to consider and reject them, either directly or indirectly through their accountable representatives in a public forum. In this respect, the creation of NICE supported the value of reciprocity by providing citizens with an example of deliberation in action in which they could assess the justifications their representatives give for policies that will affect their wellbeing in important ways. The possibility of continuing debate in Parliament about the deliberative practices as well as the decisions of NICE further helps to realize reciprocity.

The process of deliberation also has epistemic value. Decisions are more likely to be morally justifiable if decision-makers are required to offer justifications for policies to other people, including those who are both well informed and representative of the citizens who will be most affected by the decisions. The epistemic value of deliberation is especially great when the justification for a decision must combine factual and evaluative matters, as is the case with most health-care decisions, including the kind that NICE makes. Although experts may be the best judges of scientific evidence, they have no special claim to finding the right answers about priorities when degrees of risk and trade-offs of costs and benefits are involved.

Why Reciprocity Requires Substantive Principles

The practice of deliberation is an ongoing activity of reciprocal reason-giving, punctuated by collectively binding decisions. It is a process of reaching mutually binding decisions on the basis of mutually justifiable reasons. Because the reasons have to be mutually justifiable, the process presupposes at least some principles with substantive content. It is possible, and sometimes desirable, to distinguish procedural and substantive aspects of principles and theories, but to turn these distinctions into separate principles or distinct theories is to distort both the theory and practice of (deliberative) democracy. Although for convenience we refer to principles and theories as being procedural and substantive, we also claim that, strictly speaking, democratic principles and theories have both procedural and substantive dimensions, and approaches that force a sharp division are misleading.

The principle of reciprocity itself expresses neither purely procedural nor purely substantive values. A reciprocal perspective is both procedural and substantive because mutual justification cannot proceed without appealing to reasons that refer to both procedures of government and substance of laws, often at the same time. Even philosophers like Stuart Hampshire who seek to exclude substantive justice completely from their procedural political theories acknowledge the need for some substantive values—such as "common decency"—in the very concept of justice.[4] Hampshire says justice is "primarily procedural"—not entirely so.[5] Like other philosophers who want to be pure proceduralists, he never says what constitutes the correct set of procedural principles, or explains why people who remain subject to tyrannical rule should settle for only procedural principles if those permit tyranny.

At a minimum, no one would seriously dispute that justifications should recognize some of the values expressed by substantive principles, such as liberty and opportunity. It would hardly be sufficient for NICE to justify a decision to deny prescription drugs to West Indian immigrants on the grounds that they are not white. Even—or especially—if a large majority of British citizens would accept such reasoning, the justification would not satisfy any adequate standard of reciprocity. Nor would it be any more acceptable to deny prescription drugs to a disadvantaged minority on the grounds that they agreed with the conclusion. They might have agreed simply because they had less power than the groups that prevailed and had no better alternative in a bargaining situation.

To see more clearly why reciprocity requires substantive principles, we might further imagine a situation in which the process

103

of decision-making itself was fair, in the sense that the bargaining power of the parties was equitable, but in which the reasoning of the decision-makers was prejudiced (or could only be reasonably interpreted as based on prejudice) against West Indian immigrants or another disadvantaged minority group. The prejudiced reasoning then yields an outcome—supported by the vast majority—that denies critical health care to the disadvantaged minority. This outcome could not be justified on grounds of reciprocity, even if the procedures by which it was reached were otherwise completely fair. The justification for the outcome does not treat members of the minority group as worthy of a justification that they could reasonably accept. Alternatively, one might say that the prejudiced reasoning denies members of the minority group the status of free and equal persons. Given the nature of the reasoning, this would be so no matter how fair the process of decision-making itself might otherwise be.

We can see the principle of reciprocity in action, and the mixture of procedural and substantive values it implies, in the debate about NICE in the House of Commons. The debate had hardly begun when an MP (who is also a physician) challenged the idea that NICE or anyone else has the moral or political authority to ration health care. Another MP responded, saying that rationing was necessary and therefore justifiable: "Sometimes some treatments are not available when they would benefit patients or populations, because there simply are not the resources to provide all those treatments on the NHS." Although the debate at first seemed to turn on issues about the legitimacy of the process (who has the authority to decide), most critics (as well as most defenders of the Government) agreed that NICE represented an improvement as far as process was concerned. Most recognized that the new decision-making process is preferable to the old, and much superior to the less deliberative process that prevails in the United States.

The challenge instead was directed against the substance of NICE's decision in its first review of a drug. NICE had recommended against the NHS's funding the new anti-flu drug Relenza.[6] The critics worried that this decision would be a precedent that would justify NICE's recommending against funding of other, more expensive and more effective new drugs, such as beta interferon (which treats the symptoms of multiple sclerosis). The critics argued that decisions denying coverage are likely to deprive less advantaged patients of life-enhancing and life-saving treatments that more advantaged patients receive, and that this unequal opportunity cannot be justified. It leaves the less fortunate without the health care and the life chances that, if any citizens enjoy, then all should be entitled to.[7] They appealed to substantive principles, not simply to a claim that the process was unfair, or even that it was not deliberative.

Defenders of NICE's decision rightly realized that they needed to justify the substance of the decision, because the deliberative process in which NICE had engaged (and in which they were engaging in the Commons debate) could not in itself be a sufficient justification of the decision. They explicitly invoked substantive standards to defend NICE's decision. They argued, for example, that the decision not to fund Relenza would not adversely affect the basic life chances of any citizen, not even patients who are at high risk of complications from influenza. They called for more research on the effects of Relenza on high-risk patients, and suggested that if there were evidence of Relenza's benefit in reducing the serious secondary complications of influenza in such patients, then they would support NHS funding. Their arguments, whether or not correct on the merits, were entirely in order, and if correct they were also necessary to justify their conclusion. That they were necessary cannot readily be accommodated in a democratic theory that limits itself to procedural considerations.

An obvious but no less important virtue of a theory that does not limit itself to procedural principles is that, where necessary, it has no problem with asserting that what the majority decides, even after full deliberation, is wrong. Within a deliberative theory, one should be able to condemn majority tyranny on substantive grounds: one should be able to say that a majority acts wrongly if it violates basic liberty by denying health care on grounds of race, gender, or poverty. Or suppose that the majority, following perfectly deliberative procedures, decides to institute a practice of compulsory organ donation. On a purely procedural conception of deliberative democracy, this

105

law would be justified. If a deliberative theory includes substantive principles such as basic liberty that protect bodily integrity, democrats would be able to object to such a law, without abandoning their commitment to deliberative democracy.

Democrats of course may be mistaken when they assert claims based on substantive principles, either because they draw incorrect implications from a correct principle or because they rely on an indefensible principle. Perhaps compulsory organ donation does not violate basic liberty, or perhaps this particular principle of basic liberty is flawed. Our argument for including substantive principles—based on reciprocity—not only allows for both kinds of mistakes, but also incorporates into the theory itself the insight that democratic theorists and citizens may be mistaken about both procedural and substantive principles. Deliberation explicitly deals with the likelihood of mistaken views about principles and their implications, by considering the principles of a theory to be provisional, and therefore subject to ongoing deliberation. To point out the possibility of being mistaken about substantive principles is therefore not an argument against including such principles within a deliberative democratic theory.

The conclusions of purely procedural theories sometimes converge with the claims of the substantive standards that reciprocity requires. For example, a procedural theory of democracy may say that racial discrimination in voting is not justified because it excludes a class of human beings from citizenship, and this violates the procedural requirements of democracy, which demand the enfranchisement of all adult persons. This procedural reason is fine as far as it goes. But it does not go far enough in establishing why such discrimination is not justified. Democratic theorists should be able to object that racial discrimination (for example, in the provision of health care by a for-profit health maintenance organization) is not justified even if democratic citizenship or no other process values are at stake. Majority tyranny is objectionable on substantive, not only procedural, grounds.

Moreover, this kind of objection should be capable of being made from within a deliberative democratic theory. After all, democracy has never meant merely majority rule. Denying basic liberties and opportunities by racially discriminatory policies is either the result of state action or can be remedied by state action, and any such action or inaction requires a justification that could reasonably be accepted by those whose liberties and opportunities are denied. This is a direct implication of the basic requirement of reciprocity. The requirement to give such a justification—to invoke substantive principles in the public forum to justify a mutually binding law or policy—is therefore not an incidental feature of deliberative democracy. The substantive principles are integral to the deliberative process itself.

To say that the principles are integral to the process is not to deny that they may be justifiable outside of that process. Like any theorist of justice (or citizen making a claim about justice), deliberative democrats may put forward principles for consideration which they regard as justifiable—and which indeed may be correct, but simply not yet justified as laws. Deliberative theorists try to justify their substantive principles in a number of familiar ways, some just like those used by any theorist. In *Democracy and Disagreement*, we justify substantive principles such as basic liberty, first and foremost, on their own terms—by identifying core values, convictions, and paradigmatic cases where no one would reasonably deny that they were violated (for example, discrimination on grounds of race). Then by analogy and other forms of reasoning, we try to thicken and extend the principles to apply to more controversial cases. This is also how much of actual political deliberation proceeds.

Certainly, these substantive principles might be rejected, and perhaps even reasonably rejected, in a deliberative process that satisfies the procedural conditions of deliberative democracy. But a precisely parallel argument can be made about procedural principles. Procedural principles may also be rejected by a deliberative democracy (and so may a purely procedural conception of deliberative democracy). Pure proceduralists do not have access to some moral basis, which our conception lacks, on which to claim that the procedural constraints that they recommend for a constitutional deliberative democracy are correct or authoritative.

Some critics who object to including substantive principles in a deliberative democratic theory are themselves not pure proceduralists with respect to justice. They agree that justice requires the protection of basic liberties and opportunities, including perhaps even access to adequate health care. But they still insist that the subject matter of democratic theories should be kept distinct from questions of distributive justice. They are pure proceduralists with respect to democracy, but not justice. Democracy, they imply, is supposed to tell us how to decide when we do not agree on what is just; we should not confuse matters by combining principles of justice with the procedures for deciding disputes about those principles.

This argument is not so much substantive as it is definitional: democracy (including deliberative democracy) *means* fair procedures, not right outcomes. The critics cannot rely on ordinary usage, or the history of modern democratic theory, because representative democracy has rarely been characterized as exclusively procedural. Ordinary usage of a concept as complex as democracy is enormously varied, as are the conceptions of democracy found in modern democratic theory. And democratic practice itself is full of debates about substantive principles. Why then strain so hard to exclude them from the definition of democracy?

The reason cannot be that democratic theory is somehow internally inconsistent if it contains substantive as well as procedural principles. To be sure, the more principles a theory contains, the more likely there are to be conflicts among them. And including both substantive and procedural principles certainly increases the potential for conflict. But democratic politics itself is rife with conflict among principles, and a democratic theory that tries to insulate itself from that conflict by limiting the range of principles it includes is likely to be less relevant for recognizing and resolving the disagreements that democracies typically confront. When the disagreements mix substantive and procedural values as so many do in actual democratic practice, theorists who artificially segregate substance and procedure in separate theories of justice and democracy are prone to distort the role of both.

Some pure proceduralists may wish to keep out substantive principles because they are contestable, and democracy is supposed to be a means of resolving disagreement among contestable principles such as basic liberty. But the content of principles that are more procedural, such as majority rule or public accountability, is also contestable. A purely procedural theory does not avoid fundamental disagreement: conflicts among procedural principles are no less severe than those among substantive principles. For example, in the debate in Commons about NICE's decision to deny coverage for beta interferon, the MP from North Wiltshire implicitly raised a basic procedural question—to what extent does democratic control require local autonomy—when he argued that his constituents should have access to the drug. He objected that—because of the relative autonomy of regions—some citizens in other parts of the country could get beta interferon from the NHS, whereas his constituents could not. This is "a terrible tragedy for constituents such as mine, who could be prescribed beta interferon if they lived in Bath or Oxford, but not in Wiltshire."[8]

The political debates over health-care rationing that are occurring not only in the United Kingdom but also in almost every contemporary democracy clearly reveal the need to consider both procedures and outcomes in judging democratic justice. At stake are both the conditions under which these decisions are made and their content. Do the decision-making bodies bring together representatives of all the people who are most affected by the decisions? Are the representatives accountable to all their constituents? These procedural questions cannot be answered in the context of these debates without also asking: to what extent is the substance of the decisions justifiable to all the people who are bound by them? To exclude substantive criteria—such as liberty and opportunity—that judge the justice of decisions would be morally arbitrary and incomplete according to deliberative democracy's own premise of reciprocity. (To exclude substantive criteria would also be morally arbitrary and incomplete according to other premises that are often identified as fundamental to deliberative democracy, such as free and equal personhood or mutual respect.)

To affirm that a democratic theory should include substantive principles does not of course commit one to any particular set of principles. In *Democracy and Disagreement*, we propose a set of principles that are both substantive and procedural, and present arguments for their inclusion as part of the constitution of a deliberative democracy.[9] The arguments we present are intended to be part of a deliberative process itself, and in fact include fragments from actual deliberations. For example, we argue that laws or policies that deprive individuals of the basic opportunities necessary for making choices among good lives cannot be mutually justified as a principle of reciprocity requires. The basic opportunities typically include adequate health care, education, security, work, and income, and are necessary for living a decent life and having the ability to make choices among good lives. We therefore would include a principle of basic opportunity as part of any adequate theory of deliberative democracy.

Critics who object that this principle is not mutually justifiable or that other principles of equality are more mutually justifiable are effectively accepting the idea that democratic theory should include substantive principles. Even while challenging the content of the principles, these critics are nevertheless accepting the view that the terms of the argument should be reciprocal. Such challenges are welcomed by the terms of the theory itself, which asks for reasons that can be publicly assessed by all those who will be bound by them.[10] This kind of challenge can then become part of the continuing deliberative process. The reason that such a challenge fits within the terms of a deliberative theory itself is that the principles of the theory per se have a morally and politically provisional status.

Why the Principles Should Be Morally Provisional

How is it possible for a theory to propose substantive principles to assess laws while regarding citizens as the final moral judges of the laws they make? The key to deliberative democracy's answer lies in the provisional status of its principles.[11] The principles of deliberative democracy have a different status in deliberative democratic theory than they do in most other political theories. They are morally and politically provisional in ways that leave them more open to challenge, and therefore more amenable to democratic discretion. The moral basis of the provisional status of deliberative principles arises from the value of reciprocity. Giving reasons that others could reasonably accept implies accepting reasons that others give in this same spirit. At least for a certain range of views that they oppose, citizens should acknowledge the possibility that the rejected view may be shown to be correct in the future.[12] This acknowledgment has implications not only for the way citizens should treat their opponents but also for the way they regard their own views.

The process of mutual reason-giving further implies that each of the participants involved should take seriously new evidence and arguments, new interpretations of old evidence and arguments, including moral reasons offered by those who oppose their decisions, and reasons they may have rejected in the past. "Taking seriously" means not only cultivating personal dispositions (such as open-mindedness and mutual respect) but also promoting institutional changes (such as open forums and sunset provisions) that encourage reconsideration of laws and their justifications. One implication is that citizens and their accountable representatives should continue to test their own political views, seeking forums in which their views can be challenged, and keeping open the possibility of their revision or even rejection.

Deliberative democracy thus expresses a dynamic conception of political justification, in which provisionality—openness to change over time—is an essential feature of any justifiable principles. Provisionality takes two general forms. The principles are morally provisional in the sense that they are subject to change through further moral argument; and they are politically provisional in the sense that they are subject to change through further political argument.

Morally provisional principles are presented as claims that can be challenged and changed over time in response to new philosophical insights or empirical evidence, or new interpretations of

111

both the insights and the evidence. They are justified only when they are so presented. Many theories endorse something like this general outlook—for example, by adopting some form of fallibilism, or more simply by expressing general approval of moral and intellectual open-mindedness. But the provisional stance that deliberative democracy takes toward its own claims is distinctive in being integral to the theory. Deliberative democracy supports the means for fundamental change in the content of the theory itself. Deliberative democracy subjects its own principles, as well as other moral principles, to critical scrutiny over time. If as a consequence of such scrutiny, its fundamental principles substantially change—say, from a more egalitarian to a more libertarian orientation (or vice versa)—the theory is appropriately seen as undergoing revision rather than rejection.

Not all principles can be challenged at the same time from within a deliberative democratic theory, but any single principle (or even several principles) may be challenged at a particular time by other principles in the theory. Citizens and accountable officials can revise one principle in a sequential process in which the other principles are held constant. They can alter their understanding of all the principles by applying them in a different context or at a different time. For example, when the NICE board decided against funding Relenza, it implicitly made the provisional status of its decision clear by limiting its decision to a single influenza season. NICE also recommended that additional trials be conducted and further data be obtained, so that its decision could be reassessed in the next influenza season. Particular attention should be paid, the Board said, to finding out whether Relenza has positive effects on reducing serious secondary complications of influenza in high-risk patients. The moral basis for a decision against funding Relenza—the claim that the use of Relenza does not significantly affect anyone's basic opportunity in life—would no longer be defensible if evidence came to light showing that Relenza could significantly reduce serious complications of influenza in high-risk patients. In this way, both the process and the substance of the decision kept open the possibility of revising the recommendation in the future.

The possibility of revision applies not only to substantive principles but also to a principled defense of the practice of deliberation itself. This is why it is misleading to claim that substantive principles should have no place in the theory on grounds that they are merely philosophical proposals. Substantive principles are no more or less provisional—and no more or less philosophical proposals—than the case for deliberation itself. It is as possible to question, from within deliberative theory, whether deliberation is justifiable—and what it entails—as it is to question whether basic liberty is justifiable—and what it entails.

Consider the deliberation in Commons about whether NICE itself—also a deliberative forum—is the justifiable way to make health-care decisions. This part of the debate began when several MPs objected that letting NICE make recommendations is "to shield the Government from the very difficult decisions that have to be taken." Should NICE recommend beta interferon, which costs about £10,000 per patient per year and has been judged "marginally effective"? (It treats incurable multiple sclerosis "by reducing the exacerbation rate in patients who have relapsing-remitting disease without important disability."[13]) Should NICE recommend the new taxane drugs for chemotherapy, which do not cure but, as one MP put it, "can add years to life at a cost of about £10,000 per year"? If NICE recommends against prescribing expensive new drugs that can provide some health-care benefits to patients, will it thereby be shielding the Government from pressure to increase the total NHS budget? If NICE recommends in favor of the NHS prescribing these drugs, will it thereby be forcing NHS not to fund some other existing and highly valuable treatments (or pressuring the Government to increase funding for the NHS)? The answer to these substantive questions thus depends on taking a position on what the process should be.

Not even the deliberative principle that calls for giving moral reasons in politics is beyond reasonable disagreement. Some critics of deliberation argue that bargaining is not only more common but also preferable as a way of resolving moral disagreements in politics. The claim that self-interested (or group-interested) bargaining processes are better than deliberative ones relies on the premise that interest-based politics is more morally desirable and mutually justifiable than a deliberative politics. Whether political bargaining satisfies reciprocity (or any other moral standards) depends in part on the actual consequences of political bargaining in a particular social context. If those consequences can be shown to be mutually justifiable to the people who are bound by them, or at least more mutually justifiable than the consequences of deliberative processes, then to this extent substituting bargaining for deliberation would satisfy the fundamental aim of deliberative democracy. At least one claim that deliberative democrats often make about the general superiority of deliberation over bargaining would need to be revised—but revised in order to satisfy the demands of deliberative theory itself.

In any actual political context, a general defense of bargaining is not likely to be plausible. The main problem with bargaining as a general substitute for deliberation is that it accepts the current distribution of resources and power as a baseline, the place to begin the negotiations. On the face of it, this is not the best site for a moral defense of democratic procedures or outcomes.[14] It is significant that no one defending NICE's rejection of Relenza attempted to justify the decision as the outcome of bargaining. Nor did anyone in Commons suggest that bargaining should play any role in the process, as they might propose for a labor-management dispute, or a controversy about tax policy.

Is there no limit to what deliberative democrats can treat as provisional? They can encourage reinterpretations of the meaning and implications of deliberative principles, even the guiding principle of reciprocity, but they cannot accommodate the wholesale rejection of the moral justification required not only by reciprocity but many other morally based democratic theories. Deliberative democrats can welcome criticism of any of their principles, including reciprocity, but they cannot accept a general rejection of the requirement that binding political decisions must be justified by moral reasons. The refusal to give up that requirement is not peculiar to deliberative democracy. To reject the idea of moral reasoning in politics *tout court* is to abandon not only deliberative democracy, but

also any form of democracy that would claim that its laws are justified to the citizens who are bound by them. Although critics of deliberative democracy sometimes write as if they reject moral reasoning in politics, they rarely face up to what such a rejection would
entail, either in practice or in theory.

What such rejection would mean—even in a partial form in
a particular case—can be illustrated by imagining what would have
happened if NICE had made its decision about Relenza on the basis of
considerations of bargaining power. The single most powerful agent in
this case, the one that stood to gain the most from NICE's decision,
was Relenza's manufacturer and distributor, the Glaxo-Wellcome
pharmaceutical company. When Glaxo executives learned of the possibility that NICE might recommend against NHS funding of Relenza, they threatened to abandon Glaxo's operations in the United
Kingdom. They also said they would encourage other pharmaceutical
companies to boycott the British economy. As it turned out, NICE
stood its ground and Glaxo backed down from its threat. Deliberation
and justice coincided in this case, and both prevailed. That would not
have been the outcome, given the baseline distribution of power, had
NICE sought only to bargain.

Deliberative democrats thus reject—and not just provisionally—any theory that denies the need for moral justification,
and therefore also any theory that bases politics only on power. Deliberative democrats are committed—and not just provisionally—
to mutually justifiable ways of judging the distribution of power.
Deliberative democracy accepts the provisionality of its principles
but rejects the provisionality of moral reasoning itself as a way of
assessing politics. Theorists who claim that politics is only about
power must reject far more than the moral terms and the adjudica-
tive means of deliberative democracy. They must also reject criticism of any current distribution of power, however unjust it may be.
Or if they criticize it, they must do so in terms that—on their own
view—the persons who would be constrained by the power have no
moral reason to accept. If they decline to search for political principles and practices that can be mutually justified, who should listen to them? Certainly no one who is motivated to find fair terms of

social cooperation. Their audience can be only people who have themselves already given up on finding mutually defensible reasons. Those who would renounce reciprocal reasons are therefore trying either to persuade the already converted or to reach the unreasonable. In the first case their audience has no need, and in the second case no reason, to listen.[15]

Why the Principles Should Be Politically Provisional

We are now in a better position to address the second objection against including substantive principles in deliberative democratic theory—that their inclusion usurps the political authority of democratic citizens. A democratic theory that includes substantive principles can declare that a law citizens make is unjust, however correct the procedures by which they make it. It is no comfort to the defender of the authority of citizens to be told that the substantive principles are morally provisional. Even morally provisional principles—if they are the most theoretically justifiable at the time—carry the implication that they should be politically enacted. Acting on this implication denies democratic citizens the authority to determine through a deliberative process what should be politically enacted and why. To respond to this objection, deliberative democracy relies on the second kind of conditional status—political provisionality.

Political provisionality means that deliberative principles and the laws they justify must not only be subject to actual deliberation at some time, but also be open to actual reconsideration and revision at a future time. Like the rationale for treating principles as morally provisional, the justification for regarding principles as politically provisional rests on the value of reciprocity. From the perspective of reciprocity, persons should be treated not merely as objects of legislation or as passive subjects to be ruled. They should be treated as political agents who take part in governance, directly or through their accountable representatives, by presenting and responding to reasons that would justify the laws under which they must live together. We showed earlier (in "Why Reciprocity Requires Deliberation," above) why reciprocity requires actual, not merely hypothetical, deliberation. Because deliberative principles must be justified in an actual deliberative process in which citizens or their accountable representatives take part, the political authority of democratic citizens is to a significant degree respected.

But it still may be objected that once a principle or law is justified in this process, it acts as a constraint on other new laws that citizens may wish to make. Because the body of citizens and their representatives who deliberate about the new laws is never exactly the same as that which enacted the old laws, the democratic authority of citizens at any particular time is held hostage to principles justified at a previous time. Providing such constraints is of course what constitutions are supposed to do, and that may be why some deliberative democrats are wary about regarding their principles as part of a constitution. But if all the principles of deliberative democracy are seen as provisional in the sense of being open to revision over time, these constitutional constraints that embody substantive principles such as basic liberty and opportunity are not so threatening to the political authority of citizens.

Deliberative democrats do not favor continual deliberation, but they are committed not only to deliberation about laws at some time but also to the possibility of actually reconsidering them in the future. The extent to which any law is subject to actual reconsideration should depend on the strength of the available moral reasons and empirical evidence (and any other morally relevant considerations) supporting it, which often change over time. In the case of Relenza, part of the reason that NICE's decision was justified is that it called for review after a year's time, an appropriate interval in light of the significant changes that may occur over the course of even a single flu season. A decision by any official body not to fund Relenza even if otherwise well supported would not be justified without its providing for the possibility of continuing deliberation in the future. To be sure, at some point a decision is reached, as it was in this case, and it is justifiably enforced. But deliberative theory emphasizes, more than other democratic theories, what happens

117

before the decision and—even more to the point of provisionality— what happens after.

Political provisionality thus goes further than its moral counterpart. It implies that principles should be open to challenge over time in an actual political process that not only permits but encourages revision. Even when a law is rightly enacted today, the practices and institutions of deliberative democracy should ensure that it is subject to the regular reconsideration that is necessary to its justification over time. Deliberative democrats should therefore be especially suspicious of practices that routinely defer to the "intent of the framers" or that make constitutional amendments almost impossible even when the inherited reasons for supporting the laws in question are no longer compelling. Deliberative democrats should be favorably disposed toward practices that attach sunset provisions to everyday laws and procedures, and require administrators to issue periodic "impact statements" describing the effects of these laws and the regulations that enforce them. We noted earlier that the moral justification for NICE's decision against funding Relenza—the claim that the use of Relenza does not significantly affect anyone's basic opportunity in life—depends in part on evidence that the drug does not significantly reduce complications in high-risk patients. In its deliberations, NICE demonstrated its respect for political provisionality by taking specific institutional measures: limiting their decision to one flu season, providing for continuing review, and recommending further research.

The objection that the presence of substantive principles in a deliberative theory preempts democratic authority, it should now be clear, proves either too much or too little. It proves too much if the mere inclusion of substantive principles is taken to imply that these principles must therefore be politically binding on citizens. This objection would apply equally to the inclusion of procedural principles, which may be no less reasonably contestable than substantive principles. If the objection were accepted, it would require democratic theory to exclude all reasonably contestable principles, procedural as well as substantive. The objection proves too little if the complaint is only against making provisional judgments (however substantive) that challenge laws enacted by proper procedural methods. Even the critics of deliberative democratic theory could hardly fault it for rendering provisional judgments of this kind. If political theory were disbarred from offering such judgments, it would have little relevance to the democratic politics it purports to criticize.

When Moral and Political Judgments Conflict

Ideally, the moral and political judgments that deliberative democracy renders coincide. What deliberative politics decides will satisfy deliberative morality. Indeed, this happy conjunction occurs more often than is usually assumed. In the case of NICE, the decision against funding Relenza, made in a process that was more deliberative than that in which such decisions were made in the past, seems to be morally justified (at least provisionally). The most reliable studies, as reported by NICE, show that the only benefit of Relenza is a one-day reduction of influenza symptoms in the median patient at a direct financial cost to the public of as much as £10 million annually. NICE also took into account the cost of the expected increase in visits to doctors by typical influenza patients (most of whom are otherwise healthy), and the risk that the increase would overload the health-care system for a very minor health benefit. Furthermore, NICE found no evidence that Relenza reduces any of the serious, life-threatening effects of influenza on high-risk patients.

Nevertheless, there were some critics who raised reasonable moral objections to NICE's decision. In the Commons debate, the physician-MP mentioned earlier complained that the decision not to cover Relenza discriminated against poor people. "When we talk about rationing of NHS treatments, we aren't saying no one in the UK has them. What we are saying is that they aren't available to poor people. The rich and those who can afford it can get these treatments privately." The money saved for all patients would be at the expense of the poor because more affluent citizens could obtain Relenza by means of postcode prescribing.

The decision by NICE against funding Relenza would therefore at least appear to be sacrificing the welfare of some poorer citizens in order to save taxpayer money.

Whatever the merits of this MP's criticism, all parties to the dispute over Relenza should be able to agree that he has raised a serious moral question about a decision that was reached by a politically justifiable (deliberative) process. Even if, under current conditions, the NHS cannot do anything about this differential access to drugs such as Relenza, defenders of the decision (and other similarly hard choices) should be prepared to acknowledge the moral costs inherent in a situation in which rich people tend to live in richer districts that provide better health care and can also buy any health-care treatment on the market while poor people are completely dependent on the NHS for funding those treatments that may be cost-effective for society as a whole.

In this case there was some reasonable disagreement about whether the political judgment conformed to the moral judgment, but in many other cases there may be no doubt that the (procedurally correct) political judgment conflicts with the (carefully considered) moral judgment. A deliberative process that deliberative democrats recommend may yield an outcome that runs contrary to one or more of the substantive principles of justice that deliberative democrats also wish to defend. This kind of conflict does not seem to be a serious problem for a purely substantive theory, which simply declares the outcome of the process unjust. Similarly, a purely procedural theory faces no serious problem here either; it declares the outcome just, so long as the procedures were proper. But, as we have seen, a deliberative democratic theory should include both procedural and substantive principles, because the pure approaches at best neglect and at worst deny the moral complexity of democratic politics. A democratic theory that recognizes what is morally at stake in political decision-making must contain principles that are both substantive and procedural. Moreover, as we have also seen, the basic premise of deliberative democratic theory—reciprocity that calls for mutual justification among free and equal persons—supports both substantive and procedural principles.

Thus, compared to the purer theories, deliberative democracy more fully faces up to the potential conflicts between moral and political deliberation. It does not provide a simple resolution, but instead relies on deliberation itself to deal with the conflicts as they arise. But then the question persists: how can deliberative democrats affirm substantive conclusions about politics and still support the value of actual deliberation, which may or may not produce those same conclusions? Political philosophers, including deliberative democrats like us, reach substantive conclusions (including conclusions about what procedures are most justifiable) without engaging in any actual political deliberation. This seems to fly in the face of the commitment to actual rather than hypothetical adjudication of political disagreements.

Some critics pose this problem as a paradox of deliberative democracy.[16] They argue that if, on the one hand, they accept the arguments and conclusions of a substantive deliberative theory (such as the one we present in *Democracy and Disagreement*), they need not bother calling for actual political deliberation. The substantive theory provides all the reasons anyone who accepts it needs for making sound political judgments, and without the aid of any actual deliberation. If, on the other hand, critics reject the arguments and conclusions of the substantive theory, then they should also reject the deliberation that it recommends. Either way, deliberative theory that includes substantive principles seems to eliminate the need for the practice of deliberation.

As our earlier discussion of moral and political provisionality should indicate, this objection does not express a genuine paradox. The procedural and substantive principles (even the political conclusions) that deliberative democrats defend do not preempt actual deliberation. According to the very terms of the theory, the (substantive and procedural) principles and conclusions need to be subjected to the rigors of actual deliberation over time; that is part of what it means to treat them as politically provisional. (Moral provisionality also benefits indirectly from political provisionality, because individuals thinking in the privacy of their own homes or offices often draw on ideas, arguments, and perspectives—or respond

121

to challenges—that public deliberations bring to their attention.) Deliberative democrats offer their principles and conclusions not as authoritative philosophical constraints on democratic politics but as provisional contributions to democratic deliberation.

The conclusions that deliberative democrats reach about substantive and procedural principles should be understood as normative hypotheses about political morality. Given certain assumptions about reciprocity, for example, certain principles are the most mutually justifiable. The hypotheses are normative because simply showing that some people, even a majority, in fact reject the principles or their policy implications does not refute them. Restricting coverage for experimental drugs to only those who are willing to participate in random clinical trials, for example, may be the best policy even if a majority rejects it.

But the principles and policies recommended by deliberative theorists are still hypotheses, because they may be refuted or refined by showing that there are better arguments for competing principles or conclusions in the same context. And they are hypotheses about political morality—not morality in general—because their confirmation, refutation, or revision calls for public deliberation in the democratic process. Whether a normative hypothesis is confirmed, refuted, or refined, this kind of criticism can succeed only by subjecting rival arguments to the rigors of actual deliberation. Deliberative theorists should of course take into account the imperfections from which any such process suffers in practice. But so should they take account of the imperfections in their own process of reasoning, less obvious though these imperfections may be (to them if not to other theorists).

The problem of the conflict between moral and political judgment is misconceived if it is understood as requiring a choice in general or in advance between substantive and procedural principles. Both kinds of principles are subject to deliberation and are equally provisional in the way we have described. The choice between substantive and procedural principles—when they conflict— is similarly subject to deliberation and should accordingly be regarded as provisional. Neither substantive nor procedural principles have priority, even though citizens sometimes justifiably choose one over the other at some particular time.

In the debate about NICE in Commons, both the critics and the defenders appealed to both substantive and procedural principles. They addressed the justice of the decision (does it violate equal opportunity by hurting poor people?), and the process (does it insulate the government from demands to increase expenditures for health care?). Even while agreeing that the process was better than in the past, some critics challenged the substance of the decision. And even while agreeing that the substance of the decision was correct, some critics questioned the process. Some criticized, and some defended, both substance and process. But no one tried to argue that as a general rule one had priority over the other, or that the disagreement should be resolved by deciding once and for all whether substantive or procedural principles should prevail. In this respect the debate in Commons illustrated the nature of public deliberation in many of the best democratic forums. The debate also captured the moral complexity of democratic politics far better than do theories that seek to resolve the conflict of substance and procedure by excluding one or the other, or declaring one, rather than the other, trump.

Deliberative democratic theory can and should go beyond process. It can consistently incorporate both substantive and procedural principles. It should go beyond process for the many reasons that we have suggested, but above all because its core principle— reciprocity—requires substantive as well as procedural principles. Reciprocity is widely accepted as a core principle of democracy, but even those democrats who do not emphasize this principle argue from ideals such as free and equal personhood, mutual respect or avoidance of majority tyranny, which like reciprocity require both substantive and procedural principles if they are to justify the laws that democracies adopt.

Deliberative democratic theory is better prepared to deal with the range of moral and political challenges of a robust democratic politics if it includes both substantive and procedural principles. It is well equipped to cope with the conflict between substantive and procedural principles because its principles are to varying degrees morally and politically provisional. Deliberative democratic theory can avoid usurping the moral or political authority of democratic citizens—and yet still make substantive judgments about the laws they enact—because it claims neither more, nor less, than provisional status for the principles it defends.

4

Why Deliberative Democracy Is Different

In modern pluralist societies, political disagreement often reflects moral disagreement, as citizens with conflicting perspectives on fundamental values debate the laws that govern their public life. Any satisfactory theory of democracy must provide ways of dealing with this moral disagreement. A fundamental problem confronting all democratic theorists is to find morally justifiable ways of making binding collective decisions in the face of continuing moral conflict.

The solutions that most theorists propose make the problem seem more tractable than it is. Because their solutions require the rejection of rival theories, they discount much of the disagreement that gives rise to the problem in the first place. But if, as is the case in pluralist societies and in current theoretical literature, no single theory can reasonably claim to be morally sovereign, the most difficult part of the problem persists: how to deal with the moral conflict that these competing theoretical perspectives express. Furthermore, the problem is not only that the theories conflict with one another but also that fundamental disagreements arise even within a single theory.

We argue that a deliberative theory of democracy provides a different—and better—approach to this problem because it leaves open the possibility that the moral values expressed by a wide range of theories may be justifiable. On our view, a deliberative theory contains a set of principles that prescribe fair terms of cooperation.

Its fundamental principle is that citizens owe one another justifications for the laws they collectively impose on one another. The theory is deliberative because the terms of cooperation that it recommends are conceived as reasons that citizens or their accountable representatives give to one another in an ongoing process of mutual justification. Because the range of acceptable reasons is wider than that in most other theories, the principles of deliberative democracy are (in specific ways we describe below) more open to revision than those of most other theories.

To begin to show why deliberative democracy is different from other theories, and how it can more readily accommodate moral conflict, we need to distinguish between first- and second-order theories of democracy.[1] First-order theories seek to resolve moral disagreement by rejecting alternative theories or principles with which they conflict. They measure their success by whether they resolve the conflict consistently on their own terms. Their aim is to be the single theory that resolves moral disagreement. The familiar substantive views—utilitarianism, libertarianism, liberal egalitarianism, and communitarianism—are first-order theories in this sense. Each theory individually claims to resolve moral conflict, or at least to provide a basis for resolving moral conflict. Each does so in ways that require rejecting those substantive principles of its rivals that conflict with its own. But taken together they are manifestations of the problem of moral disagreement, rather than resolutions of it.

Second-order theories deal with moral disagreement by accommodating first-order theories that conflict with one another. They measure their success by the extent to which they can justify both their proposed resolutions and the moral disagreements that remain, to all who must live with them. They are called second-order because they are *about* other theories, in the sense that they refer to first-order principles without affirming or denying their ultimate validity. They can be held consistently without rejecting any of a wide range of moral principles expressed by first-order theories. Many procedural theories of democracy usually present themselves as second-order theories, because they purport to be neutral among competing substantive theories. A majoritarian theory, for example, can justify utilitarian, egalitarian, or libertarian legislation, as long as it is adopted by majority rule. But, as we shall indicate, this quality of neutrality is both undesirable and unattainable. For each procedural theory, taken individually, can produce results that are not morally justifiable, and taken together, such theories reveal substantive moral disagreements among themselves—for example, between direct and representative, populist and Madisonian, or majoritarian and constitutional theories.

Deliberative democracy is also a second-order theory, and therefore (like some procedural theories) makes room for continuing moral conflict that first-order theories seek to eliminate. But it avoids the difficulties of procedural theories by explicitly acknowledging the substantive conflicts underlying procedural theories, and by explicitly affirming substantive principles in its own theory. A full theory of deliberative democracy includes both substantive and procedural principles, denies that either is morally neutral, and judges both from a second-order perspective.

We present here, then, an argument for the distinctiveness of deliberative democracy with a particular theory of that construct in mind, one that we defend more fully in *Democracy and Disagreement*.[2] But regardless of whether this theory is accepted, the problem that this theory addresses poses a challenge that all democratic theories, whether deliberative or not, must confront. So far, none has met the challenge adequately because, in the face of competing first-order moralities, they only reiterate the conflicts that create the problem.

Democratic Responses to Disagreement

In any modern pluralist society in which people are even moderately free, there are persistent disagreements about the principles that justify mutually binding laws and decisions. Utilitarians defend maximizing social welfare, even while disagreeing among themselves about what it means and how it should be done. Should total or average utility be maximized? Does counting each person as one

127

and none for more than one also require, permit, or preclude counting each person's moral ideals and views about how others should
live their lives? Should the common currency be pleasure, preferences, or some other unit of individual satisfaction?

Libertarians defend protecting every individual's freedom
from interference, an aim that clearly conflicts with a general principle of maximizing social welfare, but just as clearly this aim is
subject to conflicting interpretations among libertarians themselves.
Persons are inviolable; they are not social resources. They own themselves, and are responsible—and should be held responsible—for
their own actions and the consequences of their actions. But what
institutions, laws, and policies respect these foundational principles
of libertarianism? Libertarians themselves reasonably disagree about
questions such as these: to what extent should parents have control
over their children's education, or to what extent should government
provide welfare for persons who may not be capable of providing for
themselves?

Libertarians unite, however, in the face of the claims of liberal egalitarians. Most libertarians would agree that the distribution
of primary goods in a society need not correct for inequalities in
natural endowments, and they therefore reject liberal egalitarian
theories that require redistribution to achieve this end. Liberal egalitarians advocate a distribution of primary goods that does not depend
on the natural endowments of individuals (it should be "endowment-
insensitive"), but they still insist that the distribution reflect free
choices of individuals as much as possible (it should be "choice-
sensitive."). Liberal egalitarians respect the capacity of individuals to
revise their ends rationally, consistent with principles of justice
that produce endowment-insensitive and choice-sensitive distributions. The foundational principles of liberal egalitarian theories are at
odds with the aim of both maximizing social welfare and protecting
every individual's freedom from interference. Liberal egalitarians also
reasonably disagree among themselves about some important basic
moral issues, including the criteria for endowment-insensitivity and
choice-sensitivity, the priority of protecting liberties over securing opportunities, and the meaning of liberty and opportunity themselves.

Communitarians also disagree among themselves, but most are skeptical about distributional principles that are sensitive to what individuals choose for themselves, whether those principles are utilitarian, libertarian, or liberal egalitarian. Such choice-sensitive principles, according to communitarians, presuppose a self that is separable from its constitutive ends. Those constitutive ends are identified with the conception of the good that prevails in a person's community, as reflected in language, religion, and other distinctive ways of life. Communitarians therefore give priority to conceptions of the good over conceptions of justice, at least those that are not grounded in a distinctive conception of the good and therefore might weaken those communal ways of life.

These theoretical disagreements are reflected in many political disputes about public policies. To be sure, most people do not hold the pure forms of these first-order theories, and many disagreements do not explicitly take the form of arguments between first-order principles. Moreover, many people hold combinations of first-order principles from different moral theories. Nevertheless, political disputes often express, in various ways, both theoretical disagreements and deep conflicts among moral principles.

Deep moral differences surface in debates between defenders and opponents of abortion, affirmative action, surrogate parenthood, capital punishment, universal health care, public and private school vouchers, unconditional and work-conditioned welfare, and many other issues of public policy. No doubt some of these disputes arise from misunderstandings, and some are motivated by bad faith and political interests. But legitimate moral differences often remain, differences that cannot be resolved without rejecting the principles of some of the first-order moral theories mentioned above. Yet no theorist has ever managed to find a way of transcending the foundational disagreements that animate many (even if not all) deep disagreements in democratic politics. Insofar as these disagreements reflect differences among first-order theories, or reasonable doubts that any single theory offers all the relevant moral insights, they will not be resolvable by appeals to any such theory.

In the absence of a single theory or set of principles that can resolve these disagreements, a first-order theorist who would apply that theory in politics is faced with two alternatives: impose the theory by authoritarian means, or submit the theory for democratic decision. The first is of course not a democratic response at all. And the second abandons any claim to be the sovereign standard for adjudicating moral conflict in politics. On this alternative, the theory becomes one of many from which citizens may choose, and the process by which they choose must become a central concern of the theory. In this way first-order substantive theories that seek political authority move toward procedural theories.

A significant attraction of proceduralism for democratic theorists is that it has the potential to avoid the choice between the stark alternatives that confront first-order substantive theories. Procedural theories do not have to claim to be capable of transcending all fundamental moral disagreements. Instead, they can try to offer a way of adjudicating the disagreements in actual politics, without seeming to commit themselves to any particular substantive theory.

But procedural theories take two different approaches here. The first is pure proceduralism, which in effect requires rejection of some substantive theories, and therefore turns out to be a first-order theory itself. Pure procedural theories compete with utilitarianism, libertarianism, liberal egalitarianism, communitarianism, and other first-order moral theories. They do not compete directly, by rejecting the first-order theories on moral grounds, but rather indirectly, by rejecting their foundations or reasons. The pure procedural form of majoritarianism, for example, presents majority rule as a foundational moral principle that answers the question: on what grounds is this law or public policy justified? Majoritarianism in this form answers this question by substituting the principle of majority rule for principles of utility, liberty, fair opportunity, or a community's conception of the good life as the moral foundation for justifying a decision, and it does so prior to any actual political decision-making. A law or policy is justified for the reason and to the extent that it is adopted by procedures stipulated by the theory.

130

This kind of proceduralism suffers from the same deficiency as other first-order theories. Because it would replace the justifications or reasons presented by some other first-order theories, it simply reproduces the substantive disagreement that created the problem of disagreement in the first place. Procedural democrats often bring substantive principles in the back door by considering them conditions of a *fair* democratic process. Procedural democrats try to limit these substantive conditions to those necessary for making the process democratic, such as free speech. But the line between what is and is not necessary is difficult to draw without invoking moral considerations, and in any case some principles, such as free exercise of religion, that any adequate democratic theory must respect do not fit within any plausible definition of necessary conditions. These procedural theories turn out on closer inspection not to be purely procedural in any significant sense that would avoid substantive moral disagreement.

Some deliberative democrats may be regarded as pure proceduralists in this sense. The procedure that fully justifies all outcomes is deliberation itself: any law enacted in a deliberative process is justified. But like most other pure proceduralists, these deliberative democrats build what are substantive values into the conditions that define adequate deliberation. On our view, these values, including the value of the practice of deliberation itself, should be made explicit, and subject to deliberative challenge. We (along with some other deliberative democrats) think it better not to characterize deliberative democracy as purely procedural.

The other procedural approach—call it conditional proceduralism—is more modest than pure proceduralism. It does not seek to replace substantive theories or their justifications. It is in this respect a genuine second-order theory. It treats procedures as instrumental to achieving substantive ends, such as stability, legitimacy, or other conditions assumed to be necessary for maintaining democratic order in the particular circumstances, but is not committed to any ends beyond these minimal conditions. A decision that conforms, for example, to the principle of majority rule is justified, but only conditionally.

131

This kind of proceduralism leaves open the possibility that the decision may be criticized as unjust because it violates substantive moral principles (a critic might argue, for example, that the injustice of the decision is weightier than whatever gain in legitimacy the decision might realize). The difficulty with conditional proceduralism is that it lacks the theoretical resources to take advantage of the possibility that it leaves open: it cannot itself support the criticism that a majority decision is unjust. What it lacks is any substantive first-order principles that would ground criticisms of the outcomes of the procedures it prescribes.

Thus both substantive and procedural responses to the problem of moral disagreement suffer from serious defects. Both fail to come to grips with the problem, either by simply reproducing the disagreement as a first-order conflict, or by resolving the disagreement in a way that violates some important first-order principles. These failures suggest that what is needed is a second-order theory (so that it does not directly reject substantive or pure procedural theories), but one with some substantive content (so that unlike conditional proceduralism it has the capacity to criticize procedurally correct outcomes). Our conception of deliberative democracy precisely meets this need: it is a second-order theory with substantive principles.

How is it possible for a theory to include substantive principles and procedural principles while still accommodating a wide range of first-order principles? The key to the answer is that the principles in a theory of deliberative democracy, whether substantive or procedural, have a different status from that of principles in other theories. Deliberative democracy does not seek a foundational principle or set of principles that, in advance of actual political activity, determines whether a procedure or law is justified. Instead, it adopts a dynamic conception of political justification, in which change over time is an essential feature of justifiable principles. The principles of deliberative democracy are distinctive in two significant respects: they are morally provisional (subject to change through further moral argument); and they are politically provisional (subject to change through further political argument).

Principles of Deliberative Democracy

The principles of deliberative democracy that we propose in *Democracy and Disagreement* (and that we believe best capture the spirit of any adequate deliberative theory) express in various forms the idea of reciprocity. The deliberative principles that flow from reciprocity provide both conditions and content for justifying laws and policies in a democracy. Reciprocity, publicity, and accountability are the chief standards regulating the conditions of deliberation. Basic liberty, basic opportunity, and fair opportunity are key components of the content of deliberation.

The basic premise of reciprocity is that citizens owe one another justifications for the institutions, laws, and public policies that collectively bind them. Reciprocity suggests the aim of seeking agreement on the basis of principles that can be justified to others who also share the aim of reaching reasonable agreement. Some first-order moralities implicitly accept reciprocity, but most do not give it the central role that deliberative democracy does. Deliberative democracy takes reciprocity more seriously than do other theories of democracy, and makes it the core of its democratic principles and practice.

Reciprocity is not foundational in deliberative democracy in the way in which first principles such as utility or liberty are foundational in first-order theories. Reciprocity is not a principle from which justice is derived, but rather one that governs the ongoing process by which the conditions and content of justice are determined in specific cases. It may be helpful to think of the process as analogous to a feature of scientific inquiry. Reciprocity is to justice in political ethics what replication is to truth in science. A finding of truth in science requires replicability, which calls for public demonstration. A finding of justice in political ethics requires reciprocity, which calls for public deliberation. Deliberation is not sufficient to establish justice, but deliberation at some point in history is necessary. Just as repeated replication is unnecessary once the truth of a finding (such as the law of gravity) has been amply confirmed, so repeated deliberation is unnecessary once a precept of justice (such as equal protection) has been extensively deliberated.

Guided by reciprocity and its fellow principles, the practice of deliberation is an ongoing activity of mutual reason-giving, punctuated by collectively binding decisions. It is a process of seeking, not just any reasons, but mutually justifiable reasons, and reaching a mutually binding decision on the basis of those reasons. It is therefore more than discussion, and it is substantive as well as procedural. Among the substantive reasons that citizens or their representatives consider in this process are some of those expressed in first-order moral theories. This is the source of the instrumental value of deliberation; its tendency to promote those values is part of what justifies the practice itself. Deliberation is valuable in part because it can encourage citizens and their representatives to invoke substantive standards to understand, revise, and resolve moral conflicts in politics. (In this respect it has epistemic as well as pragmatic value.) But these conflicts may not be, and usually are not, fully resolved, certainly not always in favor of one substantive theory. A further noninstrumental value of deliberation, therefore, is also an essential and distinctive part of any justification of deliberation. This further value is to be found in the idea of mutual respect that is part of the meaning of reciprocity. Citizens show respect to one another by recognizing their obligation to justify to one another (in terms that permit reasonable disagreement) the laws and policies that govern their public life.

Mutual respect among those who reasonably disagree is a value in itself, and in turn it has further beneficial effects for democratic politics. One of the most important effects is what we call an economy of moral disagreement. When political opponents seek to economize on their disagreements, they continue to search for fair terms of social cooperation even in face of their fundamental (and often foundational) disagreements. They do so by justifying the policies that they find most morally defensible, in a way that minimizes rejection of the reasonable positions that they nonetheless oppose on moral grounds. By practicing an economy of moral disagreement, citizens who disagree on one issue are better able to work together on other causes whose goals they share. Citizens ought to be able to agree, for example, that someone's views on abortion should not affect how she is treated with respect to other public policies. A pro-lifer ought not to favor denying a woman who has an abortion access to other essential medical care. A pro-choicer should not refuse pro-lifers the right to speak against abortion even in front of an abortion clinic.

Together with reciprocity, two other principles specify the conditions of democratic deliberation. The principle of publicity requires that reason-giving be public in order that it be mutually justifiable. The principle of accountability specifies that officials who make decisions on behalf of other people, whether or not they are electoral constituents, should be accountable to those people. Mutually binding decisions cannot be mutually justified if officials are not also accountable to what may be called their moral constituents. The moral constituents of public officials include more than their electoral constituents, and even more than citizens. They include people who are in effect bound by the decisions even though they may not have had a voice in making them. People in foreign countries who must live with, for example, the effects of toxic waste exported by our country deserve an accounting from our representatives.

The principles that define the conditions of deliberation resemble some of the principles that procedural theorists put forward. Like some procedural theories, deliberative democracy is a second-order theory. But despite these similarities, deliberative democracy, as we have already seen, is not a procedural theory. It can therefore claim two important advantages over proceduralism.

First, deliberative democracy has no problem saying that what the majority decides, even after deliberating, need not be right. A majority acts wrongly if it violates basic liberty by requiring a minority to worship as they do. Yet through a public and accountable process of fair decision-making a majority may pass a law requiring all citizens to worship in a way that conforms to their religious beliefs. On a purely procedural conception of democracy, this law would be justified. But it cannot be justified to the minority who do not share the majority's religion and whose personal integrity the law assaults. It would therefore violate the principle of reciprocity (or any ideal of treating every person as a free and equal being).

Second, when procedural theories do accept or reject an outcome favored by a first-order theory, they do so for reasons that are external to the first-order theory. They do not address that theory or its justifications on its own terms, but rather appeal to other considerations such as social stability or fairness. Although these considerations may be moral, they do not engage directly with the moral claims of the positions they reject. They therefore fail to treat their opponents with the moral respect that reciprocity requires, and they offer less scope for appreciation of opposing views and for modification of one or more of the opposing views. A procedural theory leaves the competing theories, and their political advocates, in the same moral position in which they began.

Deliberative democracy does not suffer from these difficulties, because it goes beyond proceduralism and explicitly includes substantive first-order principles. But some critics may object that by including substantive principles, the theory creates an even more serious problem for itself. They would object that a substantive principle such as religious freedom should not be part of a democratic theory. The critics would agree that religious freedom is a core part of basic liberty and should be protected. But they would argue that democratic theory should not contain any such principles, however justified the principles are on substantive moral grounds. The argument is not so much substantive as definitional: the idea of democracy refers only to procedures.

Is there any reason to define democracy so narrowly that it excludes substantive principles? The reason cannot be because the content of basic liberty or basic opportunity is reasonably contestable. So is the content of principles that are more procedural, such as publicity and accountability. Nor can it be because democratic theory is internally inconsistent if it contains substantive as well as procedural principles. There is no inconsistency in claiming that a defensible democracy must defend the religious freedom and other basic liberties of individuals, their right to vote, and to hold their representatives accountable, and that it must also find a way of fairly deciding among competing values when they conflict. Without some substantive principles deliberative democracy could not provide standards for assessing many political practices, including not only the outcomes of procedures but also the procedures themselves. Moreover, it would be morally incomplete according to its own premise of reciprocity. A democratic constitution that fails to protect, for example, the basic liberty of citizens would not be justifiable to those who are bound by it.

The three principles that provide the content of deliberative democracy—basic liberty, basic opportunity, and fair opportunity—also flow from the basic principle of reciprocity. Laws cannot be mutually justified, as reciprocity requires, if they violate the personal integrity of individuals. The principle of basic liberty therefore calls for protecting the personal integrity of each person, through such protections as freedom of speech, religion, and conscience, and due process and equal protection under the law.

Mutually binding institutions, laws, and policies that deprive individuals of the basic opportunities necessary for making choices among good lives cannot be mutually justified. Those basic opportunities typically include adequate health care, education, security, work, and income. These goods are necessary for living a decent life and having the ability to make choices among good lives. A principle of basic opportunity calls for giving individuals the capacity to make choices among good lives by providing the basic opportunities that give them such a capacity.

Reciprocity also prescribes a principle of fair opportunity, which in turn calls for nondiscrimination in the distribution of social resources that people value highly but may not be essential to living a good life or having a choice among good lives. The principle of fair opportunity rests on the reciprocal claim that discrimination against individuals on morally irrelevant grounds in the distribution of scarce social goods such as professional offices cannot be justified to the individuals who are being discriminated against.

It should not be surprising that these principles resemble those found in many first-order theories. The substantive content of deliberative democracy naturally draws on the same moral sources as other theories, and reflects many of the same conflicts that they generate. Most first-order theories also share the aim of mutual justification, at least implicitly. They only appear to reject the aim if they offer justifications for why the demands of reciprocity cannot be met in certain circumstances. If they reject the aim in principle, how can they justify imposing coercive laws and policies on citizens who reject them on moral grounds?

In trying to demonstrate the superiority of their own principles, many democratic theorists tend to emphasize the disagreements with their rivals. In contrast, deliberative democrats stress agreements, at least initially. Despite the fundamental conflicts among the theories we have noted, the points of convergence among and within competing first-order theories are substantial. Most theories either directly or indirectly defend the protection of many individual liberties, especially those that are essential to the integrity of persons (the core of the principle of basic liberty). Most theories also claim that if their principles are implemented, all persons will secure the opportunity to live a good life, an ideal that expresses the principle of basic opportunity. Similarly, most theories suggest that their principles support what we term fair opportunity.

These points of convergence provide the initial content for the substantive principles of deliberative democracy. Although other theorists sometimes seek such convergence, deliberative democrats are better situated to achieve it because they do not try to appropriate merely what they, from their own perspective, regard as valuable in rival theories. Although they do not purport to be neutral among all first-order theories, deliberative democrats do not require that competing first-order theories be rejected. Substantive principles have a different status in deliberative democracy: they are morally and politically provisional in ways that leave them more open to challenge and therefore more receptive to democratic discretion. (*On the provisional character of the principles, see chapter 3, pages 110–18.*)

Deliberative democracy is different from other theories because it contains within itself the means of its own revision. Its provisional status invites ongoing challenge to its own principles as well as those of other theories. It constructively embraces–without exalting–the moral conflict that pervades contemporary politics.

5

Just Deliberation about Health Care

W hat standards should be used to assess the process of making decisions about health-care policy? These decisions are increasingly made not only in governmental institutions such as legislatures, courts, and presidential commissions but also in HMOs, hospitals, ethics committees, review boards, professional associations, and task forces. By focusing on a case study that involves decision-makers in a for-profit HMO, we show how a theory of deliberative democracy can be relevant to institutions that make important decisions concerning health care, even when those institutions are non-governmental. We propose some generally applicable standards by which such decisions can be evaluated by both participants in the decision-making process and outsiders observing that process.

The guiding principle of deliberative democracy on which we base the standards is reciprocity: citizens and their accountable representatives seek to give one another mutually acceptable reasons to justify the laws and policies they adopt. Their aim is to justify the policies in question to the people who would be bound by them. Reciprocity sets four standards or criteria to assess decision-making about health care: the justifications that decision-makers give should consist of reasons that are accessible, moral, respectful, and revisable. This chapter illustrates how these four standards of reciprocal reasoning are applicable to the making of public policy concerning health care.

In the leading case in a prominent text on ethical issues in managed care, readers were asked to consider whether DesertHealth, a for-profit HMO, should cover a new test called PUREPAP.[1]

Approved by the FDA for assessing the efficacy of the standard Pap linear tests for cervical cancer, PUREPAP detects some of the cell abnormalities that the standard test misses. PUREPAP would benefit some individual patients but at some cost to others enrolled in the DesertHealth plan.

The case is neither dramatic in its details nor earth-shaking in its consequences, but it is therefore all the more significant, because it raises questions that are typical of the kinds of issues that health-care decision-makers increasingly—and routinely—face. What benefits should health-care plans provide and to whom? In deciding as a matter of policy what services to cover, HMO decision-makers act more like public officials than private individuals, and they face many of the same challenges that confront government, even though their decisions directly affect only those enrolled in their plan. The pattern of economic and political trade-offs that must be made and the various interest groups that must be consulted create a microcosm of the larger political process. The case can therefore help uncover a set of standards that could be used quite generally in making health-care decisions by institutions that significantly affect the health care received by individuals, whether or not those institutions are governmental.

Political theories of democracy suggest standards for assessing how these often controversial decisions can be justifiably made. The most promising theories defend a central role for deliberation in dealing with controversies such as those that characterize the making of health-care policy. These theories of deliberative democracy offer the most promising perspective for judging health-care debates because they defend a kind of politics that is explicitly designed to respond morally to moral controversies, conflicts over what count as justifiable trade-offs among valued ends or between valued means and ends. These controversies have become increasingly common in health care. Many people now recognize that more medical care is not always better. Even when it is better, its costs cannot always be justified in light of other calls on the available resources. Regardless of whether a certain kind of medical care is better on balance, it still may be desired and demanded by many people but opposed by health-care organizations concerned about cost saving.

In a deliberative democracy, citizens or their accountable representatives seek to give one another mutually acceptable reasons to justify the laws and policies they adopt.[2] These reasons are not merely procedural ("because the majority favors health care") or purely substantive ("because health care is a human right"). They appeal to principles that citizens who are motivated to find fair terms of cooperation can reasonably accept. These principles are thus both substantive and procedural.

Both the content of the deliberators' reasoning and the conditions under which they are deliberating should manifest the aim of justifying the policies in question to the people who are bound by them. This aim may never be perfectly realized in practice, but the theory of deliberative democracy offers a useful standard by which to judge actual decision-making as better or worse, to the extent that the reasons for the decisions are mutually justified.

Reciprocity, the fundamental value of deliberative democracy, is both a moral principle and a mode of justification. In general terms, reciprocity means "making a proportionate return for the good received."[3] The proportionate return for being given acceptable reasons is giving reasons in return on terms that one's fellow citizens can accept. Reciprocity is a characteristic of justice that has special force in a democracy, where people should be regarded and regard one another as free and equal members of a cooperative social system.

Reciprocity deals with disagreements in a way that expresses the equal status of citizens. Citizens are not merely objects of preference aggregation or of moral principles that others use to judge them (but that they cannot use to judge others). Citizens are active subjects who can accept or reject the reasons for mutually binding laws and policies, either directly, in a public forum, or indirectly, through their accountable representatives. Reciprocity asks citizens and their representatives to try to justify their views to one another and to treat with respect those who make a good-faith effort

141

to engage in this mutual enterprise, even when they cannot resolve their disagreements. When citizens morally disagree about public policy, reciprocity suggests that they should deliberate with one another, seeking moral agreement when they can and maintaining mutual respect when they cannot.

But deliberation that aims at mutual justification does not guarantee a just outcome. A well-designed deliberation that considers whether to fund PUREPAP may still yield the wrong answer. No decision-making process in the realm of policy-making is perfect. Deliberative democracy explicitly recognizes this, and therefore expresses a set of principles, not only a deliberative process. Those principles can help citizens and policy-makers recognize the limitations as well as the strengths of deliberation in specific contexts. The principles suggest the possibility of justifying nondeliberative means when, for example, they are necessary in order to establish the socioeconomic conditions for a decent democracy and for more deliberative decision-making.

The distribution of health care may offer an example of how nondeliberative means could, in principle, be defended by deliberative principles. Suppose that less affluent American citizens are unable either to insure themselves adequately for decent health care or to influence the political process sufficiently to overcome this inequity. This situation may be manifestly unjust by the principles of deliberative democracy. The claim of injustice would be based on reciprocity and might begin as follows: a cooperative social system operating under conditions of affluence cannot be justified to citizens who are denied the basic opportunities that decent health care affords.[4] If a nondeliberative process offers the only way to gain adequate health-care coverage for these citizens, then deliberation may justifiably be limited for the sake of furthering basic opportunity and better deliberation in the future. This argument proceeds according to the terms of deliberative democracy itself. Note, however, that the argument is hypothetical (*if* a nondeliberative process offers the only way . . . , then limitations on deliberation may be justified).

Deliberative processes are likely to work less well to the extent that the conditions under which they operate fail to treat people as free and equal citizens. When a political system is structured to give rich citizens far more political power than is warranted by their numbers or their regard for justice, then deliberative processes will suffer. Poorer citizens will have less access to decision-makers and less decision-making power than warranted. When, in addition, the government fails to secure an adequate level of basic opportunities, such as education, for all citizens, deliberative processes are likely to suffer as well.

Thus, the deliberation in DesertHealth and other HMOs and health organizations is often distorted by what might be called the burdens of injustice, the constraints that existing injustices place on what less-advantaged citizens can reasonably expect to accomplish, given their relative power. An example of a burden of injustice is that many patients today have no legal recourse against an HMO that denies them medical coverage for treatments that they, their own physician, and an independent panel of physicians all would deem medically necessary. Deliberation within one HMO is unlikely to rectify this situation for many reasons. A for-profit HMO operating in a competitive system would suffer a serious competitive disadvantage if it unilaterally extended patients' rights to include such legal recourse.

Suppose that DesertHealth refuses to cover a procedure simply because it cannot afford it, while other, better-endowed plans decide to cover it because they regard it as medically necessary. Suppose further that people who are poor through no fault of their own have access only to DesertHealth and similarly endowed plans. Under such circumstances, there is reason to question whether the basic distribution of resources for medical care in the society as a whole is just. If a deliberative process at DesertHealth concludes against coverage under these conditions, we should not blame deliberation itself. The problem is the scope of the decision: one HMO, no matter how deliberative, cannot solve the problem itself. (That is why cases limited to a single HMO cannot tell the whole story about social justice with respect to medical care.) Deliberation in a different forum may be necessary to address the problem. The best alternative to deliberation within HMOs may be publicly accountable deliberation in Congress, which has the power to set the legal parameters within which all HMOs must operate. Of course, deliberation at the Congressional level is also flawed, because of the far greater power possessed by rich citizens and insurance companies in our politics. But the question remains whether any alternative nondeliberative method of decision-making would be better in actual practice.

The imperfection of deliberation under nonideal conditions is no reason to favor nondeliberative means, unless those means can be shown to be more valuable in themselves or to promise more mutually justifiable results. Neither is generally likely to be the case. Because deliberative processes put a premium on mutual justification, they are generally more valuable than are nondeliberative means, and they are also more likely to aid victims of social injustice than are power-based processes of decision-making, such as interest-group bargaining. The participants in a deliberative process are expected to give not merely self-interested reasons for their positions, but reasons that satisfy a standard of mutual justification.

What kinds of reasons satisfy the standard of mutual justification that reciprocity requires? We focus here on four core characteristics of reasons that make them reciprocal. These characteristics provide standards for judging the reasons given for decisions about health care and the institutions within which the decisions are made.[5] (The standards should be regarded as necessary conditions, which can be satisfied to varying degrees.)

Accessible Reasons

First, the reasons that decision-makers give should be accessible. The basic rationale for this requirement is clear: to justify imposing your will on other persons, you must offer them comprehensible reasons. You would expect no less from them. The justification, if it is to be mutual, is irrelevant if those to whom it is addressed cannot understand its essential content. Simply citing a revelatory source therefore has no reciprocal value, but making an accessible argument that includes citing a revelatory source is not ruled out by this criteria. If someone says that God demands that fetal tissue not be used for research, and he also offers accessible reasons for not using fetal tissue—reasons that happen to be based on what God tells him—then it is those accessible reasons that satisfy the standard. The source of those reasons, even if inaccessible, is irrelevant to their mutual justification.

If the appeal to revealed authority is inaccessible, then why should a similar appeal to scientific authority and expertise not also be inaccessible? The conclusions and the essentials of the reasons that support scientific authority may be made publicly accessible and therefore satisfy this criterion. For example, it is perfectly legitimate for doctors to refuse to provide some kinds of treatment on the grounds that they are generally regarded—on the basis of the best scientific evidence and evaluative standards—as ineffective, medically futile, or even excessively risky. These grounds often are not purely technical or medical, because they involve the weighing of risks and benefits for the individual as well as others who might be affected, but their technical or medical aspects are critical to the justification, and they often may be difficult to explain to patients or even well-informed citizens who are not trained in medicine. Why, then, does the accessibility criterion not rule out such justifications?

Consider the justification for the decision that the benefit committee at DesertHealth is likely to make about PUREPAP. (Although the narrative of the case ends as the committee is about to make its decision, the arguments point toward a definite conclusion.) The decision the committee is likely to reach is to decline to cover this new test on the grounds that it is not cost-effective. Here is part of the reasoning (as presented by the case writer):

> PUREPAP provides a computerized rescreening process that is about 7 percent more effective in detecting false-negatives than manual rescreening of negative Pap smears. In other words, if 10 percent false-negatives are detected under the current manual rescreening system, 10.7 percent would be detected using PUREPAP. For example, if manual rescreening detected 8 false-negatives out of a 100-slide pool, PUREPAP would detect 8.56. . . . The [annual] cost to [DesertHealth] would be $4.8 million. . . . The plan's underwriters estimate that PUREPAP would cost approximately $30,000 to detect one false-negative.[6]

Ordinary patients, and even not so ordinary ones, may be excused if they do not fully follow this reasoning, but that does not

145

necessarily make the justification inaccessible. The basic conclusion can be expressed in accessible terms by clarifying what the cost means (for example by showing what other treatments might be provided for $30,000) and what the benefit actually provides (by explaining that the test only identifies abnormal, not necessarily cancerous, cells, and that those that are cancerous are likely to be picked up in time by later tests, because cervical cancer develops slowly). Behind these conclusions lie technical knowledge and some professional judgments that may not be unanimous, but this is true of many conclusions of experts that we reasonably accept in modern life.

We should not, of course, accept these conclusions uncritically. Accepting the justification for such conclusions presumes a certain amount of trust, but not blind trust. More specifically, the trust is not blind if two conditions hold. First, there is some independent basis for believing the experts are trustworthy (such as a past record of reliable judgments). Second, the experts can describe the basis for their conclusions in an understandable way. The justification would then be accessible in the way that reciprocity requires.

What kind of institutional arrangements would be likely to facilitate offering accessible justifications? Health-care decisions are best defended in forums that include representatives of the people whose health care is in the hands of the institution. The reasons are more likely to be accessible to people if accountable representatives are present when policies are being made and defended. (The consumer affairs committee in DesertHealth, which includes "consumer representatives" as well as members of the medical board, may go some way toward filling this role.) The representatives should be former or potential patients, and they should routinely be encouraged to ask critical questions and to challenge answers until the reasoning satisfies them.

In light of the generally greater power of health-care institutions than their consumer base, such institutions should also be required to give reasons for their policies to a patient tribune charged with acting more generally as an ombudsman would. Among other responsibilities, the patient tribune would make sure that the explanations the experts gave on behalf of the institution were comprehensible to the patient representatives. Representatives should have access to records of the past decisions and qualifications of the major decision-makers. Detailed technical material supporting the justification of decisions like whether to cover PUREPAP should also be available for evaluation by independent experts. Individual patients or their representatives should be able to consult independent experts as a check on the reliability of the organization's experts, whose judgment about what constitutes reasonable and affordable health-care risk may be unintentionally skewed in some way that can be discovered only by considering technical details that are beyond what patients or their representatives are able to analyze on their own.

Moral Reasons

Reciprocity demands more than accessible reasons. Self-interested reasons—or reasons that serve the interests of one's employer—are among the most conspicuously accessible. We understand only too well the argument that a policy of not covering some health-care services would increase the profits of a profit-making HMO. But reciprocity presumes a moral point of view. The reasons given must not only be accessible, they must also be moral. Thus, decision-makers should justify policies by offering moral reasons.

What counts as a moral reason, according to a deliberative perspective? The basic criterion of a moral reason, sometimes called generality, is one that deliberative democracy shares with many other moral and political theories. The criterion of generality is so widely accepted that it is often identified with the moral point of view.[7] Moral arguments apply to everyone who is similarly situated in morally relevant respects. Women who ask that DesertHealth reimburse them or their doctors for PUREPAP do not assert that only some women (or some doctors) should be reimbursed, but that all women so tested (or their doctors) should be. Similarly, the medical-policy committee that recommends against reimbursing PUREPAP does so for reasons that are general in this sense, stressing "that most cervical

147

cancer grows slowly over the course of ten to fifteen years, and . . . the implications of a false-negative are greatly overstated. . . ."[8]

Generality is not a purely formal standard, as the controversy about covering PUREPAP shows. Generality always raises a substantive question: what are the morally relevant respects in which people are similarly situated? One possible moral response to arguments for and against recommending PUREPAP for all women who have PAP tests is to recommend (and therefore reimburse) PUREPAP only for women who are shown to be at particularly high risk for cervical cancer.[9] Although this response picks out a more specific group to be rescreened and reimbursed by DesertHealth, it does so for morally relevant reasons and therefore satisfies the test of generality. A morally relevant characteristic—being at high risk for cancer—is being generally applied. As this example suggests, a reason that qualifies as moral by deliberative standards may be opposed by another moral reason. Moral reasoning therefore leaves room for reasonable disagreement because moral reasons may be multiple and may support opposing policy conclusions.

The requirement that reasons be moral distinguishes the deliberative approach from another common approach to public decision-making. That approach, based on prudence, is amoral. Prudential decision-makers give reasons that are intended to show that a policy is the best that all parties to the decision, given their relative decision-making power, can expect to achieve. Prudential reasons and their outcomes reflect the balance of power of the decision-makers. The morality of both the reasons and their results would be purely coincidental. Prudence aims not at justice (or a moral outcome), but rather at a modus vivendi, in which self-interested citizens deal with their disagreements through various forms of bargaining. Their reasoning aims at striking the best bargain for themselves, regardless of moral considerations.

The trouble with prudential reasoning as a criterion for public decision-making is that some people have far greater bargaining power than others, and prudence authorizes them to use that power in a self-interested, or group-interested, way to gain still more benefits for themselves or their group. If the managers of DesertHealth get away with offering self-serving reasons to the detriment of their patients' well-being, they should be criticized, not commended for their successful bargaining strategy. The proponents of prudence cannot justify the outcomes of self-serving reasoning to those who are at a disadvantage when the bargaining begins. What can they say to a low-income patient who is denied health care that she needs, and that would be provided if only the people in power were less powerful or less self-serving? They can suggest that she got the best deal she could in light of her relative bargaining power and their self-interested behavior. But this response gives her no moral reason to accept the decision as justified. At best, it tells her what she surely already knew: that she is the victim of an injustice because the people in power failed either to reason morally or to act morally.

Institutions should be designed to encourage more moral rather than more self-interested reasoning and action. Forums for deliberation that include representatives of less-advantaged citizens encourage decision-makers to take a broader perspective on the matters that come before them. John Stuart Mill presented one of the most cogent accounts of such a deliberative process in democracy. Participating in public discussions, a citizen is "called upon . . . to weigh interests not his own; to be guided, in case of conflicting claims, by another rule than his private partialities; to apply, at every turn, principles and maxims which have for their reason of existence the common good. . . ."[10] But deliberation will not suddenly turn self-centered individualists into public-spirited citizens. Members of the benefits committee at DesertHealth are not automatically transformed from delegates of special interests into trustees of the public interest just as a result of talking to one another. Background conditions make a big difference and need to be considered in constituting such a committee or any deliberative forum. These conditions include the level of competence (how well-informed the deliberators are), the distribution of resources (how equally situated they are), and the open-mindedness of deliberators (the range of arguments they are likely to take seriously). To urge more deliberation, we need only assume that most people are more likely to take a moral view in a deliberative process that puts a premium on moral reasoning than in a process in which assertions of political power are expected to prevail.

How can deliberative forums provide incentives for moral reasoning? These forums are likely to work best when they are designed to resemble as little as possible the processes of power politics and interest-group bargaining. Members of the committees in health-care organizations like DesertHealth should not think of themselves as merely group-interested delegates, even if they inevitably and quite properly bring different perspectives to the meetings. They should not be chosen in a way that suggests that each represents the interests of a single constituent group whose interests the representative is therefore bound to articulate and promote. A forum that is so organized is likely to replicate the results of interest-group bargaining and eschew moral reasoning. Governmental institutions should also be designed to encourage deliberation on the merits of issues rather than engage only in interest-group bargaining, which puts a premium exclusively on power at the complete expense of moral persuasion.

From this deliberative perspective, the committee structure of DesertHealth is not ideal. Separate bodies—the medical committee, the benefit committee, and the consumer-affairs committee—that each concentrate on a different aspect of policy are likely to encourage a process of decision-making that resembles interest-group bargaining. Each committee is likely to advocate a position that reflects its own special perspective or particular interest. They arrive at policy conclusions with little exposure to the perspectives or interests of the individuals represented by the other committees. To some extent, this effect may be mitigated by the overlapping membership on the consumer-affairs committee (which includes some people who are also members of the medical committee), but the consumer-affairs committee is not the final decision-making body. To promote moral reasoning, the forum in which final decisions are made should include voices that represent as many relevant perspectives as is feasible. The challenge is to make sure that many perspectives are represented without encouraging the representatives to act as mere delegates.

Respectful Reasons

One of the virtues of a deliberative conception is that it recognizes that much moral disagreement will persist even among good-willed and intelligent people. Some of the moral disagreement that persists in politics is reasonable: moral positions conflict, and there is no morally definitive perspective that, for public purposes, settles the disagreement. Health-care policy poses some of the most intractable of these issues. Should individuals be held responsible for health problems that are partly the product of their own choices? Should children who cannot give informed consent ever be subjects of experimental medical research? These questions have moral answers, some of which each of us is able to offer. From a public perspective, the problem is that our answers, more often than not, conflict, and some of the conflicts will be moral and reasonable.

In the face of disagreement of this kind, a deliberative conception specifies a third criterion of reasoning that strives for reciprocity: the reasons that decision-makers give should be mutually respectful of those who are similarly striving for mutual respect. Mutual respect demands more than toleration or a benign attitude of indifference toward others. It requires a favorable attitude toward, and constructive interaction with, people with whom one reasonably disagrees when those persons are similarly willing and able to adopt such an attitude. In respecting one another as moral agents, participants in a deliberative process recognize the difference between morally respectable differences of opinion and merely tolerable ones. Differences that represent morally respectable conflicts are what we call deliberative disagreements, conflicts in which citizens seek a resolution that is mutually justifiable but continue to differ about moral principles or their practical implications.

Many disputes over how much emphasis to place on individual responsibility for certain health-care problems and how much of the cost of their health care consumers therefore should be required to bear through higher insurance premiums are examples of deliberative disagreements, because conflicting sides can justify

151

their views as reasonable within a reciprocal perspective. Consider, by contrast, a dispute in which some people defend de jure racial segregation or discrimination against non-Christians. This would be an example of a nondeliberative disagreement because one side can be rejected as unreasonable within a reciprocal perspective.[11] These positions reject the very premise of reciprocity, the idea that mutually binding laws and policies should be mutually justified to the people who will be bound by them. De jure racial segregation and discrimination against non-Christians cannot be justified to those who are severely disadvantaged by these policies.

The criterion of mutually respectful reasoning helps distinguish a reciprocal perspective from another kind of moral perspective, which bases itself on the criterion of impartiality. Reciprocity stands between prudence, which demands less from justifications, and impartiality, which demands more. Impartiality insists that reasons be impersonal. It requires citizens to suppress their own personal perspectives and partial projects when setting social policies and procedures. The prime example of an impartialist approach is utilitarianism. In practice, it favors expert decision-making and implies that the medical professionals in DesertHealth should have the final say as long as their judgment is consistent with general professional opinion. The preferred impartialist method is neither bargaining nor deliberation, but demonstration, which aims as far as possible to establish the truth of a comprehensive moral view. In the face of moral disagreement, impartiality tells citizens and officials that they should affirm the view most consistent with the true morality as determined by impersonal justification. There is no further moral need for mutual respect or for actual political deliberation.

The trouble with impartiality is that it does not take moral disagreement seriously enough. More precisely, it fails to provide a satisfactory way to deal with the moral disagreements that inevitably remain on many issues when expert opinion on the technical and medical problems or the demonstration by a comprehensive moral philosophy such as utilitarianism are complete. In the face of a fundamental moral disagreement such as funding fetal-tissue research, expensive organ transplants, or experimental diagnostic tests such as PUREPAP, the impartialist approach can declare only one side (or no side) correct. If one side is correct, it provides no reasons for recognizing moral value on the other side. It therefore offers no way, other than agreement, for the other side to respect the decision on moral grounds.

In a deliberative process characterized by mutual respect, participants recognize the moral merit in their opponents' claims (insofar as they have merit). Such a process can help clarify what is at stake in a moral disagreement by encouraging deliberators to sort out self-interested claims from public-spirited ones and to recognize those public-spirited claims that should have greater weight. Through a deliberative process, participants in a health-care forum can isolate those conflicts that embody genuinely incompatible values on both sides. Conflicts that do not involve such deep disagreement can then easily be addressed and may turn out to be more resolvable than they at first appeared. Some may be the result of misunderstanding or lack of information, and some may be appropriately settled by bargaining, negotiation, and compromise. In this way, deliberation can use moral principles to put moral bargaining, negotiation, and compromise in their place.

In the face of deliberative disagreements, deliberative democracy recommends what we call an economy of moral disagreement. In justifying policies on moral grounds, citizens should seek the rationale that minimizes rejection of the position they oppose. By economizing on their disagreements in this way, citizens manifest mutual respect as they continue to disagree about morally important issues on which they need to reach collective decisions.

The economy of moral disagreement can be seen at work, for example, in two bodies that considered the issue of fetal-tissue research, the Warnock Commission in England and the Fetal Tissue Research Commission in the United States. Both commissions sought to focus on those issues and justifications for positions that would help them reach some reasonable consensus, rather than on those that were more likely to produce polarization. To the extent that they recognized and respected one another's conflicting values, commissioners helped realize the potential for mutual respect among citizens. Even when decision-makers cannot responsibly avoid highly contentious issues, they can manifest mutual respect by seeking to help participants understand the perspectives of their opponents. The respectful quality of the reasoning that decision-makers present—for example, how well they recognize the competing values at stake—has value in addition to that of the conclusion they reach.

An economy of disagreement is sometimes appropriate even when one side of the dispute seems mainly economic. In the dispute at DesertHealth, some patients and their doctors argued that any decision not to cover PUREPAP would be discriminatory. The money saved for all patients would be at the expense of the health of women. The decision would at least appear to be sacrificing lives of some women for improving the health care of men (and, of course, some other women). In the spirit of economizing on moral disagreement, the consumer affairs committee recommended that the plan spend the resources that would have been spent on PUREPAP instead on a program to promote regular Pap tests, which not only would be more cost-effective but would also be nondiscriminatory.

Suppose, for the sake of argument, that spending more on Pap smears would be more cost effective than funding PUREPAP, and suppose that the consumer affairs committee had not recommended that the money saved be used to fund more Pap smears so as thereby to help improve women's health. Or suppose the management of DesertHealth rejected the consumer affairs committee's recommendation with no comment. In either case, advocates of funding PUREPAP could reasonably have thought that DesertHealth was putting profit-making above concern for women's health. Regardless of whether a decision not to fund PUREPAP was right, a defense of DesertHealth's decision—however accurate on the narrow merits—would have failed to appreciate the value of respectful reasoning and the correlative practice of economizing on moral disagreements. Mutually respectful reasoning may not always achieve the right results, but neither will bargaining or impartialist reasoning.

Although economizing on moral disagreement may reduce moral conflict, it does not eliminate disagreement. Indeed, in the process of clarifying and identifying moral differences, it may intensify the conflict. Some critics of mutual respect therefore may object that deliberative practices raise the moral stakes. Suppose DesertHealth rejected the recommendation of its consumer affairs committee and refused to spend the money saved on PUREPAP on improving women's health care. The internal conflict might have become greater than it would have been without any internal deliberative body. DesertHealth might have rued the day it instituted a consumer affairs committee. Critics are correct in suggesting that, in some contexts, the effort to economize on moral disagreements may turn what would otherwise be a simple bargaining situation into a conflict of moral principle, and thereby encourage no-holds-barred opposition and political intransigence. Moral sensitivity sometimes makes necessary political compromises more difficult. But moral sensitivity often exists even without deliberative practices. When moral sensitivity exists (about the neglect of women's health-care needs, for example), a bargaining situation may blow up in the face of the winners. Just as important, the absence of moral reasoning in bargaining situations makes unjustifiable outcomes and compromises more common.

What is even worse is a public philosophy that simply accepts unjustifiable outcomes and inequitable compromises, because it assumes that self-interested bargaining is the best that politics in our society has to offer. If a disagreement about a change in eligibility for health care turns only on the question of costs, nothing is gained by invoking principles of justice and benevolence. But when a dispute raises serious moral issues—the avoidable deaths of less-affluent patients or the exclusion of certain groups, such as immigrants, for example—then it is not likely to be resolved more satisfactorily by avoiding arguments that are both moral and mutually respectful. Most disputes in health care raise serious moral issues and therefore put a social premium on the parties' mutually seeking an economy of moral disagreement.

As they debate the future of health care in this country, members of Congress would be well advised to adopt this practice, at least upon occasion. If Republican and Democratic senators, for example, could economize on their moral disagreements about patients' rights in managed-care plans, citizens would be considerably better off than they are today. A moral compromise in this spirit would also signal that the parties were willing and able to put bipartisan concern for improving the welfare of Americans above partisan bickering.

Revisable Reasons

Like most case studies, the story about DesertHealth is presented as if the protagonists were making a one-time decision: Should they fund PUREPAP or not? This approach may be appropriate for pedagogical purposes, but it is a misleading guide for the practice of deliberation. A fundamental feature of deliberative reasoning is that its conclusions are morally revisable over time (what we also call "provisionality"). If the benefit committee decides not to cover PUREPAP, DesertHealth officials should ensure that opportunities remain open to challenge, and to a reversal of the decision, in the future in light of new scientific information, fresh understandings of the moral values at stake, and other changes in the context within which the decision is made.

The revisable status of justifications is implied by the value of reciprocity. Decision-makers owe justifications for the policies they seek to impose on other people. They therefore must take seriously the moral reasons offered by their opponents. If they take seriously their opponents' moral reasons, they must acknowledge the possibility that, at least for a certain range of views, their opponents may be shown to be correct in the future. This possibility has implications not only for the way citizens should treat their opponents, but also for the way they should regard their own views. It urges them to continue to test their own views, seeking forums in which their views can be challenged, and keeping open the possibility of their revision or even rejection. (The same obligation to justify policies that are imposed on other people supports the practice of the economy of moral disagreement described earlier.)

Deliberative forums that deal with moral disagreements put a premium on presenting justifications in a way that can stand the test of new moral insights, empirical evidence, and alternative interpretations of insights and evidence. Many other theories, of course, endorse something like this general outlook—for example, by adopting some form of fallibilism or, more simply, by expressing general approval of moral and intellectual open-mindedness—but the revisability that deliberative democracy recommends even for its own basic claims is integral to its substantive conception of justice. Deliberative democracy welcomes fundamental change in the content of the theory itself. This includes revisions, reinterpretations, and even rejections of its own principles. It also includes changes in the meaning and implications of a mutually justifiable deliberative process. All of these possibilities are consistent with—indeed they follow from—the fundamental idea of reciprocity: mutually justifying that which is mutually binding to the people who are most affected by the decision.

The purpose of revisability is not only to respect the moral status of the participants in the process, but also to improve the quality of the decisions they make. Revisability offers important protection against the mistakes that citizens, health-care professionals, and administrators all inevitably make. Ideally, all the participants recognize that their reasons and conclusions are revisable, but even when some or all of the participants do not recognize this before they deliberate, a well-constituted deliberative forum can foster revisability and its recognition. The give-and-take of moral argument in deliberative forums that reconsider existing laws and policies and propose new ones assumes revisability. Participants have an incentive to learn from one another, to recognize their individual and collective misapprehensions, and to develop new views and policies that can more successfully withstand others' critical scrutiny. When citizens bargain and negotiate, they may learn how better to get what they wanted to begin with, but when they deliberate, they can expand their knowledge, including their self-understanding of what is best for them and their collective understanding of what will best serve their fellow citizens.

The most important implication of the revisability criterion for health-care institutions is that decision-making bodies should be designed so that their conclusions are regarded as provisional and therefore revisable over time. Medical findings that are relevant to health-care decisions change rapidly and sometimes dramatically over time. The economic conditions of society that are relevant to the resources available to health-care institutions also vary. What counts as adequate health care changes with objective as well as subjective social conditions, and changes in one institution, such as government policy, are very relevant to other institutions, such as nonprofit and for-profit HMOs. At any given time, deliberative forums must, of course, reach conclusions, but the conclusions should always be open to challenge in a subsequent round of deliberation. Deliberation continues through stages as various health-care officials present their proposals, consumers respond, officials revise, consumers react, and the stages recur. This is what we call the reiteration of deliberation, which also recommends deliberative democracy and makes it more suitable to decision-making under conditions of shifting uncertainties.

The distribution of health care is not the only issue that could benefit from such reiterated deliberation. When, if ever, is medical experimentation justified in the absence of informed consent? On what basis should organs for transplantation be allocated? Do physicians have a duty to treat AIDS patients? And, of course, should DesertHealth cover PUREPAP? The list of contestable questions could be expanded almost indefinitely. For a start, consider the variety of topics covered in the "Questions for Consideration" at the end of each chapter in the casebook from which we took the DesertHealth case. Because moral disagreement in decisions about health care is not likely to diminish, the need for more and better deliberation is likely to grow.

If the values of deliberative democracy are to be more fully realized in the practices of health-care forums, the justifications that the decision-makers give should be more accessible, moral, respectful, and revisable. To the extent that the institutions for making these decisions are deliberation-friendly in these ways, the decisions that they produce will be more mutually justifiable, and the health-care policies they represent will be more morally legitimate, even if they are not always politically popular. By making the process in which citizens decide the future of their health care more deliberative, they stand a better chance of resolving some of their moral disagreements, and living with those that will inevitably persist, on mutually acceptable terms.

6

The Moral Foundations of
Truth Commissions

As South Africa's Truth and Reconciliation Commission (TRC) began its public hearings, the newspaper *The Sowetan* warned, "Reconciliation that is not based on justice can never work."[1] The paper was expressing not only a widely shared doubt about this particular commission, but also the most commonly voiced objection to truth commissions in general. Whether or not the South African effort at reconciliation will work, this commission, like other such institutions in other countries, carries a heavy moral burden. By the terms of their charters, these commissions sacrifice the pursuit of justice as usually understood for the sake of promoting other social purposes, such as establishing historical truth and effecting social reconciliation. The pursuit of justice does not presuppose a retributive view of punishment. It only means bringing individuals to trial who are credibly alleged to have committed crimes, and seeking a legal verdict and an appropriate punishment if they are found guilty. Still, in a democratic society, and especially in a society that is trying to overcome injustices of the past, trading criminal justice for a general social benefit such as social reconciliation requires a moral defense if it is to be acceptable.

Many proponents of truth commissions accept the burden of providing such a defense and try to offer, explicitly or implicitly, moral justifications for these institutions and the practices that they support, such as the granting of amnesty in exchange for full testimony, which the South African commission had the power to grant. We shall argue, however, that the three most common justifications of truth commissions are incomplete from a democratic perspective.[2] Each captures one part of the moral case for truth commissions, but only one part. We incorporate these parts into a consistent democratic perspective that offers a more complete set of criteria for justifying truth commissions. A justification for these commissions is more adequate, according to these criteria, the closer it comes to meeting three moral challenges that justifications of public institutions should try to satisfy in a democracy. And the closer that a truth commission comes to meeting these three moral challenges, the more it can contribute, both instrumentally and by its very example, to the democratization of its society. We suggest that commissions and citizens can promote this process by practicing an economy of moral disagreement, in which they seek common ground where it exists, and maintain mutual respect where it does not.

First, the justification should be moral *in principle*. It should explicitly appeal to rights or goods that are moral and therefore are comparable to the justice that is being sacrificed. The stability of a political regime is not itself a moral good or a sufficient reason to sacrifice justice for individuals. A stable regime can be unacceptably repressive. Social stability counts as morally relevant only when it is part of what justice (or some other moral good) requires. Those who defend the aims and activities of a truth commission must distinguish a moral justification from a purely prudential or self- or group-interested one. It offers a threshold criterion, asking us to distinguish moral reasons from amoral or immoral reasons.

Second, the justification of a truth commission should be moral *in perspective*: it should offer reasons that are, as far as possible, broadly accessible and therefore inclusive of as many as possible of those who seek moral terms of social cooperation. The reasons should be accessible not merely to certain groups or individuals within a society but to all citizens who have a legitimate interest in living together in one society. This requirement of inclusiveness does not mean that everyone must actually approve the justification, only that the justification cannot reasonably be dismissed out of hand by people who seek moral terms of cooperation. This challenge is created by the need for citizens of a morally pluralistic democracy to work together in seeking fair terms of social cooperation. Because it offers an ideal of accessibility that rarely if ever can be met completely, the justification should not be expected to be accessible to everyone, even to everyone who seeks moral terms of social cooperation. A truth commission should be judged, on this criterion, by how broadly accessible and inclusive it is, taking into account the social context within which it operates (including the history and ongoing legacy of injustice).

Third, the justification should be moral *in practice*: it should offer reasons that are, to the extent possible, embodied or exemplified by the commission's own proceedings, and are not intended to be put into practice only by other institutions, observers, and future governments. This requirement is all the more important to the extent that the victims of past injustices reasonably perceive that some significant part of justice—such as just punishment for the crimes committed against them, their families, and fellow citizens— is being sacrificed in order to create the truth commission. Some other significant part of justice, therefore, should be realized now in the ongoing activities of the truth commission. This justification goes further than merely suggesting that in some general way the commission will help society move beyond the injustices of the past or will serve as a means to a better democracy in the future (though showing both can be an important part of any adequate justification). The justification of the commission is more fully moral and more adequate to the extent that the means themselves used by the commission exemplify the justice that is being pursued. Otherwise, the moral foundation will look dangerously like that which could be offered by any regime that tries to justify current violence and injustice in the name of a promise of future peace and pursuit of the general interest. The more closely connected the practices of the commission are to the character of the democratic government to which citizens aspire, the more adequate its justification.

In analyzing the moral foundations of truth commissions, we use the South African experience as our paradigm. Although the analysis is relevant to many other such commissions, the TRC, we believe, is the most appropriate example because it is the most comprehensive in its purposes and procedures. It was charged with a wide range of responsibilities, including providing an accurate account of atrocities, granting amnesty to those who confessed to their role in political crimes, and making recommendations for reparations. The commission had subpoena power and took testimony in public (unlike some commissions, such as the Chilean one, in which victims and perpetrators testified in private). We cannot offer anything close to a full analysis even of the South African case. A more complete analysis of any single case would require further refinement and quite possibly revision of the more general criteria and arguments that we present here in light of the many relevant particularities of the society. But any more comprehensive analysis that included a moral justification of the commission in question would need to be guided by general standards.

The Moral Burden

The power of South Africa's TRC to grant amnesty to political leaders, security officials, and other individuals who confessed to committing political crimes during the apartheid regime was a political compromise between the advocates of total amnesty and the proponents of criminal prosecution. This "truth for amnesty" provision, added in the so-called "postamble" to the interim constitution, is thought by many people, including many victims of apartheid, to be the most morally problematic practice of the TRC. Although only a relatively small proportion of applicants were granted amnesty, some were among the most egregious perpetrators. When amnesty is granted, the guilty not only go unpunished, but even escape trial. When amnesty is not granted, prosecution of the applicants is still possible but has proved difficult.

Some defenders of the TRC deny that this consequence threatens justice. They suggest that the guilty would go unpunished in any case, and that there is therefore no sacrifice of justice. Although they are right to doubt any standard that would suggest that perfect justice could be done without a truth commission, they cannot sustain the claim that the "truth for amnesty" provision entails no sacrifice of justice whatsoever. They cannot be sure that all of the guilty parties would in any case go unpunished. (In fact, not all have gone unpunished in South Africa.) Nor can they escape the moral burden of justifying the trade-off that any proposal entails between various valuable ends of justice in the context of an ongoing society in which many crimes against humanity have been committed by members of that society. The moral burden of justifying a truth commission that adopts the "truth for amnesty" provision therefore still remains, even if it is lessened by the recognition that the alternative is a trial that does not completely satisfy the ideal of criminal justice.

Other defenders who deny that the "truth for amnesty" provision threatens justice argue that the aim of the commission should be understood as "achieving *justice* through reconciliation."[3] Rather than abandoning justice, the commission actually promotes an "enriched form of justice." By forcing citizens today to "face the horrors of the past," it helps to overcome the "indebtedness" owed to the victims of apartheid. Acknowledging past wrongs and especially repudiating wrongful judicial verdicts certainly may be part, even a necessary part, of achieving justice now.

But these measures are not enough to constitute criminal justice as it is commonly understood, and the defenders of this view do not demonstrate that the common conception of justice should simply be abandoned, rather than outweighed or overridden by more urgent moral considerations. Justice is not achieved when a murderer or rapist publicly acknowledges his crimes but is not brought to trial and suffers no further punishment. (This is true whether one believes that the aim of criminal justice is retribution, deterrence, rehabilitation, or some other purpose.) Even if the victims received financial compensation, the demands of justice (on virtually any theory of punishment) would not be satisfied. Nor would the kind of public shaming that perpetrators were said to experience in testifying to the commission count as satisfying justice.[4]

It may be true that most victims of apartheid who have testified before the TRC have not sought prosecution of the perpetrators.[5] But it cannot be assumed that the views of the testifiers are representative of the average black South African or even the average victim of apartheid (a category that includes most black South Africans).

Some people who deny that justice is being sacrificed appeal to other moral values, such as a greater need to recognize "systemic and collective evils" rather than individual piecemeal wrongs, and the importance of furthering the "efforts to strengthen democratic institutions."[6] But these arguments are seriously incomplete if they do not come to terms with the moral cost of sacrificing ordinary criminal justice, even while recognizing that it could be realized only imperfectly in a nonideal society. Indeed, in a nonideal society, truth and reconciliation also can be realized only imperfectly. For example, even a simple institutional compromise such as the separation of the Amnesty Committee from the other sections of the TRC, which caused the commission's final report to be issued long before the Amnesty Committee had finished its work, meant that much of the truth presented to promote reconciliation was not based on truth revealed in exchange for amnesty. If proponents of justice through reconciliation believe that the ordinary conception of criminal justice is completely misguided or inappropriate in a particular context, they need to develop their argument much further than they have done.

The reaction of the families of Steven Biko and Griffiths Mxenge, prominent murdered heroes of the antiapartheid movement, brings out vividly why the moral burden of sacrificing criminal justice should not be ignored. Both families vehemently opposed the creation of the TRC because they believed that it would prevent justice from being done. "[Some people] say that offering amnesty helps the truth come out," says Mhleli Mxenge, Griffiths' brother. (Griffiths Mxenge, a human rights lawyer, was brutally assassinated by the counterinsurgency police unit.) "But I don't believe that knowing alone makes you happy. Once you know who did it, you want the next thing—you want justice!"[7] The family members believe they are speaking not only for victims and their families but also for other citizens who care about seeing justice done. Further-more, because the TRC did not observe the customary rules of evidence and the deliberate procedure of criminal process, both victims and perpetrators understandably complained that their due-process rights were violated.[8]

The Realist Response

The question remains: Can this sacrifice of justice be justified? A common answer takes what may be called a "realist" approach. Realists do not deny that terrible injustices were committed by many people under apartheid and that they should be condemned. But some realists argue that because the injustices were so widespread and systematic (indeed *because* they were so terrible), it is not practical to prosecute individuals for the crimes. The evidence, they argue, would be difficult if not impossible to discover in many cases; many guilty people would escape, and some innocent people would be punished.[9] The acquittal of former Defense Minister Magnus Malan in 1996 was widely seen as demonstrating that former officials could not be prosecuted successfully. The only hope of finding out what happened in the past would be to encourage the guilty to come forward voluntarily, which they would not do if they faced the prospect of a trial and punishment. The "truth for amnesty" provision itself was a necessary political compromise, without which the new constitution could not have been put into effect. Furthermore, that provision does not rule out prosecution of those who refuse to apply for amnesty or who fail to receive it.

The emphasis of this realist justification seems to suggest that moral considerations are irrelevant, or at least unrealistic. Insofar as a realist response denies the relevance of moral considerations, it fails to meet the first and most basic moral challenge. In addition to its neglect of moral considerations, there is also an internal problem with the realist response. Its emphasis on political necessity itself is not as realistic as it purports to be. It is realistic to suppose that bringing most or all of the perpetrators of political crimes to justice is impossible. But it is not realistic to dismiss as impossible the goal of bringing *some* perpetrators to justice, at least in societies like South Africa, where extensive records were kept, and where a relatively reliable police force and criminal justice system are now in place.

Shortly after Malan was acquitted, Eugene de Kock, the former head of Vlakplaas, a notorious police hit squad, was convicted on eighty-nine charges, including six counts of murder, and sentenced to two life terms, the maximum allowable under South African law. (In mid-1999, the TRC granted de Kock amnesty for one of his offenses.) Giving up on the goal of punishing as many of the perpetrators of political crimes as possible is not an inevitable conclusion; it is a political decision with moral implications, and therefore one that needs to be morally justified. Furthermore, the TRC considered but rejected a less punitive alternative—lustration (denying perpetrators the opportunity to hold public office)—which would have fallen short of satisfying criminal justice but could have gone some way toward fulfilling its underlying aims.[10]

One way to begin morally justifying the decision to forgo prosecution is to argue that even under the relatively favorable conditions of criminal justice that exist today in South Africa, the perpetrators who would most likely be brought to justice would have been lower-level rather than higher-level officials, those who committed lesser crimes under apartheid. Some defenders of the TRC make this argument and suggest that such selective enforcement would itself constitute an injustice of a serious sort. This is a credible starting point for justifying the "truth for amnesty" provision, but it should not be confused with a realist justification. It invokes a moral argument, which suggests that punishing only the lesser crimes of apartheid is worse than punishing no crimes of apartheid at all.

When defenders of the South African commission offer a moral justification for forgoing some prosecutions that would otherwise be possible without the "truth for amnesty" provision, they implicitly recognize the limitations of a realist defense, which relies on necessity rather than morality. To say that bringing any perpetrators of political crimes to justice is impracticable, and that therefore a truth commission is the best available alternative, is an abuse of the argument from necessity; it is also a non sequitur. Even if bringing any perpetrators of political crimes to justice were impossible, it still would not follow that setting up a truth commission would be preferable to other alternatives. The past wrongs could be acknowledged, and society could find many other ways to move forward effectively, without forcing citizens to endure the painful and divisive testimony produced by a truth commission. Many conservative white South Africans and conservative black supporters of the Inkatha Freedom Party voice this view. In the words of an Inkatha politician from Umlazi: "It's just opening old wounds. It makes you hate the person you had forgiven."[11] The view requires a response that goes beyond what the realist offers.

A moral argument is implicit in any defensible claim that a truth commission is the best realistic alternative to seeking justice. If the only goal were to preserve the present political regime and move forward with the practical business of government, a truth commission could be as much an obstacle as an aid to this goal. The beginning of a moral argument is implicit in at least some forms of the realist justification. The incipient argument is that a truth commission should help citizens move ahead together to establish a new society based on commonly shared values (which of course need not be universally shared).

But the goal of creating a society with commonly shared values still lacks moral content and therefore cannot justify the sacrifice of criminal justice. At minimum, the content of the new society's shared values must be incompatible with continuing the morally abhorrent practices of the past. The simple idea of a commonly shared set of values cannot justify anything, certainly not giving up the pursuit of justice. No one should reasonably expect the families of Biko or Mxenge to accept this conclusion if its main justification has so little (if any) moral content. They, along with all victims of apartheid, present strong arguments in favor of pursuing justice against those who committed crimes under apartheid. Their arguments deserve a moral response, one that is more specific than the hope of building a better democracy. Even if some kind of amnesty were necessary to bring the constitutional negotiations to

168

a successful conclusion, this political compromise must itself be shown to be moral compromise. Otherwise, the new democracy will be morally flawed from its inception.

A more specific response is offered by those who argue that a truth commission can help establish not just peace but a decent peace and a minimally decent society.[12] Although this response is sometimes identified as "realist," it runs against the realist response to the extent that decency is identified with specific moral standards such as securing basic liberties and a decent standard of living for all individuals. (To the extent that decency is left undefined, the response suffers from the same problem as holding out the general hope that the commission will build a better democracy.)

Proponents of a decent society generally presume some moral standards, thereby rejecting the realist's morally indifferent response to the critics of truth commissions. The standards, which may be similar to those of deliberative democracy that we defend below, pay homage to the antirealist idea that any adequate justification must assume that seeking shared principles is morally desirable, and further that it is more morally valuable than prosecuting the perpetrators of past political crimes. But these assumptions in turn depend on showing that the principles being sought and the means of seeking them have substantial moral value that was absent from (or less present in) the old society. Otherwise, there is not sufficient moral value to counter the considerable moral cost of granting amnesty to perpetrators of past political crimes.

The realist justification becomes acceptable only if it takes on greater moral content. Specifically, what it needs is an account that would show how the process of a truth commission itself can help create a more just society. The shared principles that are being sought for the future must be moral in principle; they must address the legitimate concerns of all members of society; and they must be closely linked to the practices in which the commission is engaged. Insofar as these conditions are satisfied, the realist justification is compatible with the more complete justification we shall suggest below. It provides the missing moral principles, perspectives, and practices for a truth commission.

169

The Compassionate Response

Another common defense of truth commissions adopts the perspective of the victims. Some proponents of this defense follow a therapeutic approach, pointing to the psychological benefits of offering public testimony and receiving public confirmation of injustices.[13] Others take a more theological approach, focusing on the value and meaning of acts of forgiveness and repentance. Archbishop Desmond Tutu, the chair of the TRC, has emphasized Christian forgiveness as a great value of the body's proceedings. He connects this Christian idea to the secular goal of the commission—reconciliation—which is part of its legislative mandate. Other commentators have suggested a similar but more secular version of this idea: the commission enables victims to choose to "fulfill the civic sacrament of forgiving."[14] Taken together, these justifications have been identified, by Tutu and others, as a conception of "restorative justice."[15]

Restorative justice remains relatively undeveloped as a conception of justice, but Archbishop Tutu and other proponents explicitly offer a moral justification for forgoing the conventional justice of holding the perpetrators of apartheid legally responsible for their crimes. The justifications that make up this approach share a compassionate concern for the victims of apartheid and their families, those individuals whose interests, they recognize, were unjustly sacrificed to apartheid.

In caring about the disadvantaged, these justifications certainly live up to the first challenge: they invoke a genuinely moral principle. Yet the question remains whether truth commissions actually serve the victims who testify before the commission as well as these justifications claim. If they do, it is also important to ask whether restorative justice's emphasis on the perspective of the victims who testify before the commission meets the second challenge, which seeks an inclusive perspective shared by all those citizens who are willing to live on fair terms of social cooperation with others. In addition, it is important to ask to what extent these justifications live up to the third challenge: do they link the practice of showing compassion to victims who testified before the TRC with the far more inclusive practices of a democratic government that the country is seeking to build, one that will not be oriented primarily toward demonstrating compassion for victims of apartheid?

The TRC heard the testimony of more than 2,000 victims of apartheid-era brutality, and received written submissions from more than 23,000 people. Although the testimony helped establish and publicize the wrongs committed under the previous regime, it was also intended to help the victims and their families find some relief and redemption from their suffering. Many welcomed the chance to testify, and said they experienced some relief and less hostility toward their former oppressors. But in many other cases, testifying reopened old wounds, produced continuing psychological stress, and generated hostility toward the new government and the TRC itself. Officials of the Trauma Center for Victims of Violence and Torture, a nongovernmental group that provides services in the Cape Town area, reported that 50 to 60 percent of the victims they had seen suffered serious difficulties after giving testimony.[16] The TRC was rightly criticized for failing to provide adequate counseling and other concrete support to victims. But such support should be provided to *all* victims, not only those who testified, and therefore should not be considered part of the justification for the distinctive mission of the commission.

The theological version of the compassionate defense does not promise psychological relief, but instead offers the possibility of a deeper kind of spiritual satisfaction that some find in the act of forgiving. The difficulty is that many victims do not share Archbishop Tutu's Christian faith, and even those who do may hold a different view about the appropriateness of forgiveness in such situations. One can grant that on at least some major interpretations of Christian morality, forgiveness may enhance the virtue of granting amnesty, and perhaps may even be obligatory. But those who endorse this interpretation should also grant that many sincere and reasonable Christians do not share their interpretation. Nor is it shared by many other religious or secular moral understandings that also deserve respect.

Boraine, the deputy chair of the TRC, recounts the reaction of a South African woman to the testimony by the killer of her husband:

> After learning for the first time how her husband had died, she was asked if she could forgive the man who did it. Speaking slowly, in one of the native languages, her message came back through the interpreters: "No government can forgive." Pause. "No commission can forgive." Pause. "Only I can forgive." [Pause.] "And I am not ready to forgive."[17]

Does anyone have compelling reasons, let alone the authority, to tell this women that she should forgive the man who abducted and killed her husband?

Proponents of forgiveness do not insist that victims be compelled to forgive their oppressors, only that the TRC provide an opportunity for them to do so. Moreover, most of the perpetrators who confessed probably did not expect (and should not have expected) their victims to forgive them. Dirk Coetzee, a commander of Vlakplaas, South Africa's counterinsurgency police unit, testified that he ordered the assassination of Mxenge. Speaking to the commission, he said, "I will have to live with my conscience for the rest of my life and with the fact that I killed innocent people." But then he added: "In all honesty, I don't expect the Mxenge family to forgive me."[18]

With the perspective of other citizens and the aim of the future democratic government in mind, we must ask whether, even if many victims would choose to forgive, it is desirable for them to do so. South Africans of differing perspectives can respect Archbishop Tutu's call for forgiveness without agreeing that they have an obligation to forgive their oppressors, or even that the commission would best serve South Africa by encouraging the victims of apartheid to forgive. Many citizens (including the victims themselves) may reasonably believe that it is morally inappropriate to forgive people who are unwilling to be punished for their crimes, or unwilling to offer their victims restitution. Many may also reasonably think that although forgiving does not logically entail forgetting, it makes forgetting much easier, and the crimes of apartheid should not be made easier to forget. Making the memory of the crimes of apartheid less vivid runs the risk of bringing about similar crimes in the future, and in itself fails to show the respect for the victims that is their due.

Crimes like those committed under apartheid are acts not only against particular victims but also against society and state. Like the victims of crimes, so too do society and state have something to forgive. Although forgiveness by a state institution such as a truth commission is logically possible, it is not desirable from a democratic perspective, independently of forgiveness by the victims themselves. The crimes of apartheid constitute an affront to the basic democratic principle of treating all adults as free and equal citizens. A post-apartheid state that forgave these crimes could not credibly claim to be committed to the most basic democratic principles.

What sense of "restorative justice," if any, can be achieved by a post-apartheid state that (rightly) does not insist on forgiving the crimes of apartheid? Some proponents of restorative justice suggest that the wrongs committed under apartheid can be transcended by the practices associated with a truth commission. But this suggestion is sometimes tied to a more modest claim: that by respecting the voices of victims who testify to the crimes committed under the apartheid regime, and providing reparations, a truth commission can help restore public recognition of the humanity of apartheid victims. These are worthy moral aims of a commission, but they are not sufficient to support claims of transcendence, upon which the conception of restorative justice seems to be based.

One source of the insufficiency of these aims is their failure to address the reasonable claims by some victims that restoration is impossible with amnesty, and that there are alternative ways in which the voices of victims could be heard and reparations granted without offering amnesty to the perpetrators of apartheid. Proponents of restorative justice should recognize that for many victims of apartheid, restoration is incompatible with amnesty, and perhaps unachievable in any case.

Even if restoration is not the best way of justifying the work of a commission, a commission's practice of giving public voice to victims can still be viewed as an important component of a more comprehensive justification. The goals of a commission may be more forward-looking, more political, and more inclusive than those that are conveyed by the restorative notions of forgiveness, therapy, and reparations for the victims who testify.[19] In the South African case, restorative justice seems to elevate these aims above those of establishing a more democratic society for all South Africans who are willing to recognize the reasonable demands of a democracy. The latter aim is more inclusive, even of the perspectives of victims, many of whom can neither forgive nor forget. It is also more inclusive of the perspectives of those perpetrators of apartheid who recognize the heinousness of their crimes and therefore do not (and should not) expect to be forgiven.

The aim of reconciliation, part of the TRC's formal charge, therefore does not have to be understood as requiring forgiveness by either victims or the state. If "the healing of the nation" is taken to mean forgiveness by the victims and repentance by the perpetrators of apartheid crimes, it is a utopian aim, and not even a positive one.[20] The aim of reconciliation should not be seen as seeking some comprehensive social harmony, whether psychological or spiritual. As one commentator on the South African experience observes, "Taken to the extreme, the reconciliation of all with all is a deeply illiberal idea."[21] Reconciliation is an illiberal aim if it means expecting an entire society to subscribe to a single comprehensive moral perspective.

Reconciliation of this comprehensive sort is also deeply undemocratic. A democratic society should indeed seek reconciliation on some fundamental matters of political morality, such as freedom of speech, press, and religion, equal political liberty, equal protection under the law, and nondiscrimination in the distribution of social offices. But a democratic society that strives for a consensus on such fundamental matters of political morality must recognize that moral conflict in politics more generally cannot be overcome or avoided. In the democratic politics that the new South Africa seeks, a substantial degree of disharmony is not only inevitable but desirable. It can be both a sign and a condition of a healthy democracy.

The Historicist Response

A third kind of justification takes a more impersonal point of view and finds the value of truth commissions in their contributions to establishing past facts and acknowledging past wrongs. The discovery of historical truth is seen as both an end in itself and a means to a better society. The point is not so much to help the victims but more to create a shared history as a basis for social and political cooperation in the future. Facing unwelcome truths, demonstrating the illegitimacy of apartheid, decriminalizing the resistance movement, forging a collective memory—these are among the many aims embraced by historicist justifications.[22]

Although the historicist justification emphasizes truth, it tries to accommodate the aim of reconciliation. Some writers interpret reconciliation *as* a form of establishing the truth. They suggest that reconciliation should be understood as "a closing of the ledger book of the past . . . like the accountant's job of reconciling conflicting claims."[23] As du Toit puts it: "a conscious and justified settling of accounts with the past."[24]

The collective memory created by settling accounts in this way is partly a culmination of a political struggle. Collective memory, Foucault writes, is a "very important factor in struggle . . . if one controls people's memory, one controls their dynamism. . . . It's vital to have possession of this memory, to control it, administer it, tell it what it must contain."[25] Although Foucault may exaggerate the extent to which collective memory can be created and controlled by any regime, such memory can play an important role in consolidating the power of a newly emerging democracy, just as it helps sustain authoritarian regimes.[26] But the more attractive aspect of this justification is the use of its moral condemnation of the past as a way to start developing some common moral standards for the future. The "conscious and justified settling of accounts with the past" becomes a deliberate and worthy way of establishing democratic norms for the future.

On this interpretation, the historicist response invokes moral principles, in accord with the first requirement of justification.

Some critics, however, may still object that it does not satisfy the second requirement: it fails to support a sufficiently inclusive perspective, because the history on which it relies favors the victors over the vanquished in the recent struggle against the apartheid regime. The violence perpetrated by the previous regime is treated more harshly than the violence committed by resistance fighters.

Far from being a weakness of the historicist justification, this asymmetry of criticism of pro-apartheid and anti-apartheid activists is a strength. It is a reasonable response to the challenge of relying on an inclusive moral perspective. An inclusive perspective does not demand neutrality with respect to all sides in a moral conflict. If the cause of one side is more justified than the other, any "settling of accounts" should acknowledge that asymmetry. That the cause of anti-apartheid activists was just does not excuse, let alone justify, all their actions, as the TRC explicitly acknowledged.[27] But that does mean that the activists' actions are appropriately judged in a more favorable moral light than the actions of the defenders of the apartheid regime. This kind of moral judgment is one that could not reasonably be rejected even by those who once participated in the apartheid regime, if they were motivated to find a perspective that could be accepted in principle by their fellow citizens.

The major weakness of the historicist justification is its failure to live up to the third challenge, which asks that the practices of the commission itself exemplify the practices of the democratic government toward which the society is striving. Despite the concessions and qualifications that the historicist defenders may offer (the evidence is imperfect, the conclusions are fallible, and so on), their *aim* is for a truth commission that comes as close as possible to a conclusion that expresses the collective, authoritative version of what happened and how it should be judged.[28] The standard historicist justification implies that there is a truth about the past to be finally discovered and authoritatively acknowledged. This truth, moreover, is not merely factual but also evaluative.

The aim of truth-seeking, with its strong intimations of singularity and finality, is not the most appropriate model for political judgment in an emerging democratic society. In most such societies—South Africa perhaps most of all—moral divisions in politics will persist, and deep disagreements about fundamental values will not be resolvable by political processes. The political institutions of a pluralist democracy must find ways to cope with a persistent disagreement in which no side can be shown to be either right or wrong, in many relevant respects. The practice and culture of such a democracy must make room for a wide range of continuing conflict, even while trying to contain it within the bounds of civility. Civility does not require being friendly or even polite to one's oppressors, but it does call for respecting people as civic equals with whom one has politically deep but reasonable disagreements.

The assumption of ongoing disagreement and continuing conflict differs from the usual model of the aim of most truth commissions, which in this respect behave more like judicial proceedings. A commission typically seeks a historical verdict, a final judgment about what happened, intended to be accepted by all citizens. A truth commission that modeled the democratic society it is trying to build would be more welcoming of controversy. It would avoid final judgments where the available evidence or arguments were still uncertain. It would explicitly acknowledge its own limitations, as the South African commission did in a remarkable section of its *Final Report* entitled "The Commission's Shortcomings."[29] A democratically oriented commission would, most of all, exemplify how people can live with continuing disagreements about what exactly happened in the past and why, and still respect each other as fellow citizens.

Such a commission would not need to assume that truths about the past are impossible to discover, only that many of the truths that we can find now are tentative and many other truths that we are likely to find in the future are better sought by encouraging conflict and controversy, rather than by establishing a politically authoritative consensus. Even some of the defenders of the TRC who emphasize the importance of seeking a consensus on truth recognize the limits of this quest: they describe the primary function of the commission as expressing "unwelcome truths . . . so that inevitable and

177

continuing conflicts and differences stand at least within a single universe of comprehensibility."[30] Comprehensibility of conflicting claims is far less final than reconciliation, and far more accepting of the kind of continuing moral controversy that is not only inevitable but desirable in a democracy.

Democratic Reciprocity

Democracy is the most familiar and now the most justifiable way of dealing with such disagreements in politics. Basic to all moral conceptions of democracy is the idea that people should be treated as free and equal citizens, and should be authorized to share as equals in governing their society. All moral conceptions of democracy therefore defend universal suffrage; free and fair competitive elections; the right to run for public office; freedom of speech, press, and association; and due process and equal protection under the law, along with other civil, political, and socioeconomic rights that are necessary conditions for effective political liberty. Public institutions such as truth commissions must also be morally justified to the citizens on whose behalf they act.

In justifying truth commissions in a democratic context, we rely on a conception of deliberative democracy. Deliberative democracy offers the most promising perspective by which to judge the work of truth commissions that engage in public deliberations because, more than other conceptions of democracy, it defends a deliberative politics that is explicitly designed to deal with ongoing moral controversy.[31] At the core of deliberative democracy is the idea that citizens and officials must justify any demands for collective action by giving reasons that can be accepted by those who are bound by the action. When citizens morally disagree about public policy, they should deliberate with one other, seeking moral agreement when they can, and maintaining mutual respect when they cannot.

The fundamental value underlying this conception is reciprocity, which asks citizens to try to justify their political views to one another, and to treat with respect those who make good-faith efforts to engage in this mutual enterprise even when they cannot resolve their disagreements. Reciprocity also calls for establishing social and economic conditions that enable adults to engage with each other as civic equals. To the extent that those socioeconomic conditions are absent, as they are to varying extents from all existing democracies, a conception of deliberative democracy offers a critical perspective on socioeconomic as well as political institutions.

Even when there is no better alternative to deliberation over ongoing disagreements in nonideal contexts, deliberation does not present itself as a panacea. A deliberative conception of democracy also recognizes the limitations of deliberation in specific contexts. A deliberative conception and deliberation itself can justify using nondeliberative means, for example, when such means are necessary to establish the socioeconomic preconditions for a decent democracy and more deliberative decision-making.

Even under the best conditions, deliberation is not a substitute for deciding, and deciding is not a substitute for deliberation. The two go together, and together they are the most morally powerful combination that a democracy can offer to justify its political decisions to the people who are bound by them. A deliberative democracy helps avoid tyranny by recognizing that a vote alone, even that of the vast majority, cannot justify a decision as being substantively correct. But a deliberative democracy also recognizes that deliberation is no substitute for action, and that deliberating before deciding is no guarantee that the action taken will be the right one. But deliberation does encourage attention to relevant values, and to this extent it increases both the legitimacy of democratic decision-making and the likelihood that the decision will be a morally reasonable one.

There is certainly a broad scope for reasonable disagreement about how much deliberation is sufficient, whether a particular instance of deliberation is as good as it can be, and whether the ensuing decision is just. But "sufficient," "as good as it can be," and "just" are ideal standards, and failing to meet them does not render a deliberative decision illegitimate. Democratic institutions, practices, and decisions can be judged as more or less legitimate to the extent that they are supported by reciprocal reasons, reasons that can be accepted by those who are bound by them.

To the extent that a truth commission seeks to provide reciprocal reasons, it fulfills the requirements for moral justification. First, reciprocity is not only a moral principle but also an important aspect of justice.[32] Moreover, it is a characteristic of justice that has special force in democratic politics, where citizens must cooperate to make their lives go well, individually or collectively. Other citizens make their claims on one another on terms that each can in principle accept. Because this kind of exchange is itself a form of justice, a truth commission that strives for reciprocity directly addresses the challenge posed by the sacrifice of other kinds of justice.[33] Even if the question remains whether reciprocal justice should take precedence over these other kinds of justice, a justification based on reciprocity engages this moral challenge on its own terms.

The standard of reciprocity also satisfies the second requirement of justification by providing an inclusive perspective. A reciprocal perspective is one that cannot reasonably be rejected by any citizen committed to democracy, because it requires only that each person seek terms of cooperation that respect all as free and equal citizens. It does not require that all citizens accept as morally correct the conclusions of any commission or even the laws and policies of any democratic government now or in the future. Reciprocity is a principled perspective that allows for a wide range of reasonable disagreement. South African citizens should be able to agree that apartheid was wrong (because it did not respect all South Africans as free and equal citizens). They should also be able to recognize that many legitimate institutions, such as the legal system, and many professionals, such as lawyers, were implicated to varying degrees in the apartheid regime.[34] But they may reasonably disagree in many cases about the extent to which particular individuals should be held responsible for apartheid's crimes, and about what particular policies would best alleviate its effects.

A commission that accepts reciprocity as a justification also practices what it preaches about the democratic society that it is trying to help create, thus responding to the third challenge of justification.

Reciprocity serves as a guide not only for a future democracy, calling on citizens to justify their political views to each other, but also for the commission itself, calling on commissioners and testifiers to practice some of the skills and virtues of the democratic society they are striving to create. The commission thereby applies to its own proceedings one of the most basic principles that any future democratic society should follow. The openly participatory process by which members and staff of the TRC were appointed, and the generally public process in which its proceedings were conducted, demonstrated its own commitment to democratic practices. More generally, sincere efforts on the part of citizens to offer an account of their political past closely resemble the most basic activities in the kind of democratic politics to which a healthy democracy aspires: sharing one's political point of view with one's fellow citizens in an effort to persuade them at least of its reasonableness, and potentially of its rightness. The very activity of providing an account that other citizens can be expected to understand as reasonable (even if not right) indicates the willingness of citizens to acknowledge one another's membership in a common democratic enterprise. This is an important part of any ongoing democratic project, and therefore a step toward a democratic future in deeply divided societies.[35]

A truth commission that succeeds in eliciting reasonable accounts of the past from citizens cannot of course claim to have achieved a democratic transformation of society, because reciprocity in its fullest form demands much more than that. But even in this incipient form, a commission that proceeds in this spirit exemplifies the value (and limits) of the democratic virtue of mutual respect among people who deeply but reasonably disagree.

The Economy of Moral Disagreement

One of the most important implications of democratic reciprocity for the conduct of truth commissions, as well as for democratic politics, is what we call the principle of the economy of moral disagreement.[36] This principle calls on citizens to justify their political positions by seeking a rationale that minimizes rejection of the positions they oppose. Following this principle, citizens search for significant points of convergence between their own understandings and those of citizens whose positions, taken in their more comprehensive forms, they must reject. By economizing on their disagreements in this way, citizens manifest mutual respect as they continue to disagree about morally important issues on which they need to reach collective decisions. The meaning of the economy of moral disagreement can be seen more clearly by comparing its demands with those of the three other responses we considered above.

The effort to economize on moral disagreement is no less realistic than the realist's recommendation to set aside justice for the sake of stability and to get on with the business of government. Indeed, the economizing itself can contribute in significant ways to more effective politics, as citizens look for common ground and learn to respect the divisions that remain. Only if citizens economize on their moral disagreements is it realistic to expect the development of minimally decent societies—which eschew systematic violence and repression and secure the most basic liberties and opportunities for their members—in nations such as South Africa.

Furthermore, reciprocity is as realistic as it is moral, in the sense that it does not require that citizens seek points of convergence with people who are unwilling to reciprocate. In societies as deeply divided as are South Africa and other countries that have created truth commissions, any absolute demand to economize on moral disagreement, regardless of the motivation or actions of one's political adversaries, would be not only unrealistic, but also undesirable. Victims of injustice should not be expected to economize on their disagreement with perpetrators of the injustice unless the perpetrators of the injustice demonstrate a willingness to assume responsibility for their actions. Reciprocity does not require agreement for its own sake. It advocates finding *moral* grounds for agreement. While acknowledging the exigencies of practical politics emphasized by the realists, the principle of the economy of moral disagreement provides a critical standard that adds moral content to political judgments and encourages moral distinctions in the exercise of official discretion.

A commission that seeks to economize on moral disagreement will not grant blanket amnesty. In exercising their discretion, commissioners can demonstrate respect for those who reasonably disagree with them about the relative value of reconciliation and justice by refusing to grant amnesty for the most egregious crimes. A prime example is the case of de Kock, the Vlakplaas commander. Commonly referred to as "Prime Evil," de Kock was convicted of committing crimes, most of which "had little or nothing to do with politics, and others [that] were heinous in the extreme."[37] Unlike some other former apartheid officials, de Kock had done nothing to aid the anti-apartheid movement. He seems indeed a fitting candidate for punishment. (Although he received amnesty for some of the crimes for which he was convicted, he remains in prison serving a life sentence.)

Archbishop Tutu reminded those who criticized the commission's grants of amnesty that the perpetrators of injustice "are still in the security forces and part of the civil service. These people have the capacity of destroying this land. . . . If there were not the possibility of amnesty, then the option of a military upheaval is a very real one."[38] However true this may be in general, each specific appeal for amnesty needs to be considered on its own merits. Rejecting the request for amnesty of an official like de Kock, who represents an extreme in both his criminal actions and his eagerness to escalate the atrocities of apartheid, is a way that commissioners can demonstrate their respect for critics' desire for justice while maintaining a commission's forward-looking commitment to furthering the cause of democracy in South Africa.

While the principle of economizing on moral disagreement is more demanding than what the realist response requires, it is less demanding than what the compassionate response suggests. It does not require repentance and forgiveness, which seem to ask citizens to learn to love their political adversaries. "[O]nly love has the power to forgive," Hannah Arendt wrote. And, "Love, by its very nature, is unworldly, and it is for this reason rather than its rarity that it is not only apolitical but antipolitical."[39] But while reciprocity does not aim at encouraging love among citizens, it does aim at developing some degree of respect among citizens. "[W]hat love is in its own, narrowly circumscribed sphere," Arendt concluded, "respect is in the larger domain of human affairs." Respect is less personal than love. It does not require intimacy or closeness, or even an admiration of a person's achievements or particular qualities. Respect is a civic acknowledgment: the recognition that others are our fellow citizens and that we are willing to treat them as such, as long as they demonstrate a willingness to reciprocate. This degree of reconciliation would be a great accomplishment in the South African context, a more political and potentially inclusive achievement than providing psychological or spiritual redemption for some victims. It would also take a great deal of political effort, especially on the part of those South Africans whose past actions have demonstrated disrespect and even contempt for their fellow South Africans.

Although respecting one's fellow citizens does not require repentance or forgiveness, the deliberations of truth commissions encourage citizens both to recognize and to acknowledge the extent to which repentance and forgiveness are valued by their fellow citizens. Deliberation therefore accommodates values that are central to the compassionate response. Many victims have said that all they want is to tell their story and to have their husband's body exhumed for a decent burial. Having heard the perpetrators testify to horrendous crimes against their loved ones, some of the same victims want something significantly more—reparations and justice in the form of punishment of the perpetrators. An important advantage of a deliberative democratic perspective is that it respects all of these responses, even in the same person. The practice of economizing on moral disagreement does not decide in advance which of many reasonable responses is appropriate. Economizing on moral disagreement also has the potential for accommodating a diverse set of demands, even beyond those that are central to the more compassionate response of restorative justice.

Economizing on moral disagreement does not require that a commission or citizens try to reach consensus on comprehensive conclusions about the past, as the historicist response usually does. That principle leaves more questions open to further dispute and discussion than does the project of determining and acknowledging the truth about apartheid and its victims. Citizens who try to economize on moral disagreement may acknowledge the seriousness of judgments of their fellow citizens without necessarily accepting all the judgments as true. They may, for example, regard the judgments as plausible, worthy of further consideration, and even potentially justifiable, without actually endorsing them.

The willingness to testify to crimes committed and to crimes endured, on the one hand, and the willingness to consider seriously the testimony of one's fellow citizens, on the other, constitute an important part of the process of a truth commission that seeks to realize reciprocity. When citizens take each other's testimony seriously, they evaluate the credibility of its content and the credibility of those who are testifying. A fair evaluation requires the open-mindedness to consider the merits of the testimony of those who testify. This kind of open-mindedness is the same quality that makes it possible for citizens of a democracy to respect and to learn from their disagreements.

Unlike a trial that depends on making a definite binary choice between guilt and innocence, a truth commission can encourage accommodation to conflicting views that fall within the range of reasonable disagreement. The justification that we develop here favors such accommodation, a practice that itself is an exercise in democratic politics. It suggests how a truth commission can express respect for differing points of view without either endorsing them as clearly correct or rejecting them as clearly incorrect. It then becomes the responsibility of both the participants and the observers to determine, through ongoing public deliberation, which points of view fall within the range of reasonable disagreement.

This range is not unlimited, and citizens, especially leaders, need not be hesitant about rejecting views that they believe lie outside it. Archbishop Tutu and some senior ANC officials rejected as unreasonable the written testimony of former president de Klerk, which accompanied his apology to citizens who had suffered the atrocities of apartheid. In his testimony, de Klerk insisted that he was unaware of a long succession of killings, bombings, and tortures by high-level officials in his own party and government. He claimed that these were "the criminal actions of a handful of operatives of the security forces of which the [National] Party was not aware and which it would never have condoned."[40] Tutu had reasonable grounds to deny this claim, because he had personally told de Klerk at the time about some of these crimes. Although because of a court challenge the commission withheld its conclusion about the individual responsibility of high-level officials, this particular dispute should have been resolved on empirical grounds. Both sides of the controversy had access to the relevant evidence, and both de Klerk and Tutu accepted the moral assumptions about official responsibility that were relevant to resolving this case. This dispute therefore does not lie within the range of reasonable disagreement.

Reciprocity does not demand moral detachment. Economizing on moral disagreement is completely compatible with taking a strong position against apartheid, even raising vigorous objections against individuals and groups that supported the apartheid regime. The economizing that reciprocity recommends is a moral practice, governed by moral principles that would condemn injustices and would judge unjust actions harshly and praise just ones. Nevertheless, a commission inspired by this kind of reciprocity would also call for testimony from the leaders of the resistance to the unjust regime (in South Africa, those who fought apartheid). It would ask these leaders to acknowledge their violations of human rights, as the TRC did, much to its credit, though not without provoking political criticism and legal challenge by the ANC and its supporters. Demanding such an acknowledgment does not entail deciding whether fighting the injustice of apartheid justified the violations of human rights, as in the case of ANC bombings of innocent civilians. The point of the acknowledgment is to demonstrate respect for those innocent individuals who were killed in the anti-apartheid cause.

A truth commission economizing on moral disagreement can also encourage attitudes and actions that go beyond mutual respect. It offers the victims of injustice a forum for demonstrating an even stronger form of civic magnanimity, a benevolence that leads to accepting the perpetrators of injustice as civic equals. Because this benevolence is supererogatory, a truth commission cannot expect all or even most victims of injustice to display it. But the TRC was neither foolish nor utopian to think that such benevolence is possible. Its prime model no doubt was President Nelson Mandela himself.

Shortly after he was released from prison, Mandela gave several remarkable speeches in the spirit of reconciliation, none of which showed any signs of bitterness toward his oppressors, nor any intention to seek retribution. When asked how he could be so magnanimous toward his oppressors, Mandela replied, "I could not wish what happened to me and my people on anyone." Surely no one should expect such magnanimity from anyone who has suffered the injustices that Mandela and many other South Africans have suffered at the hands of their own countrymen. But to the extent that the TRC not only officially elicited but also publicly recognized the benevolence of citizens who suffered the injustices of apartheid, it secured a better future for South African democracy.

Even the less demanding virtues of democratic reciprocity would, if more fully realized, help build a stronger democracy in South Africa, as well as in other countries seeking to overcome the legacy of unjust regimes. Truth commissions alone cannot overcome that legacy. The full realization of deliberative democracy—or for that matter the full realization of a minimally decent democracy—presupposes social and economic conditions that neither South Africa nor any other democracy can yet possess. Truth commissions, we have suggested, can constructively contribute to this process of democratization and, as important, can help constitute it. Commissions that respect the principles of deliberative democracy provide a cogent response to the moral challenge of their critics, a fruitful guide for their own conduct, and a robust justification for their moral foundation. Neither truth nor justice alone, but a democracy that does its best to promote both, is the bedrock of any worthy truth commission.

Notes

Chapter 1
What Deliberative Democracy Means

1. For a sample of the debate, see Iraq War Debates 2002–03, University of Michigan Document Center http://www.lib.umich.edu/govdocs/iraqwar.html. Two of President Bush's key speeches were: "President Bush Outlines Iraqi Threat," 7 October 2002, The White House, http://www.whitehouse.gov/news/releases/2002/10/20021007-8.html; and "President Delivers the State of the Union," 28 January 2003, http://www.whitehouse.gov/news/releases/2003/01/20030128-19.html. For a critic's speech, see Senator Robert C. Byrd, "Rush to War Ignores the U.S. Constitution," 3 October 2002, http://byrd.senate.gov/byrd_newsroom/byrd_news_oct2002/rls_oct2002/rls_oct2002_2.html [accessed 4 January 2004].

2. Jean-Jacques Rousseau, *Du contrat social*, in *Political Writings*, vol. II, ed. C. E. Vaughan (Cambridge: Cambridge University Press, 1915), Bk. II, ch. 3; Bk. IV, ch. 1. Rousseau worried that if citizens were to come together in the assembly to discuss what the general will should be, they would be tempted to make compromises, and perhaps even form factions which by their nature do not express the general will. A modern, less extreme version of this view (which does not rule out public deliberation) is developed by Robert Goodin, who argues for what he calls "deliberation within," not because he fears factional politics but because he thinks any other kind of deliberation is impractical in large-scale democracies [*Reflective Democracy* (Oxford: Oxford University Press, 2003)].

3. Although this definition is intended to capture what we believe to be the essential characteristics of deliberative democracy, deliberative democrats disagree among themselves about many of its features. For a recent sample of the disputes and other conceptions, see James Bohman and William Rehg, eds., *Deliberative Democracy* (Cambridge, Mass.: MIT Press, 1997); Jon Elster, *Deliberative Democracy* (Cambridge: Cambridge University Press, 1998); Stephen Macedo, ed., *Deliberative Politics* (Oxford: Oxford University Press, 1999); John Dryzek, *Deliberative Democracy and*

Beyond (Oxford: Oxford University Press, 2000); David Estlund, ed., *Democracy* (Oxford: Blackwell, 2002); and Frank Cunningham, *Theories of Democracy* (London and New York: Routledge, 2002), pp. 163–83.

4. Thucydides, *Peloponnesian War*, S. Lattimore, trans. (Indianapolis: Hackett, 1998), II. 40.

5. Aristotle, *Politics*, in *Complete Works*, vol. II, J. Barnes, ed. (Princeton, N.J.: Princeton University Press, 1984), Bk. III.

6. Edmund Burke, *Burke's Politics*, R. Hoffman and P. Levack, eds. (New York: Knopf, 1959), p. 115.

7. Joseph Bessette, *The Mild Voice of Reason: Deliberative Democracy and American National Government* (Chicago: University of Chicago Press, 1994), p. 13.

8. John Stuart Mill, *Considerations on Representative Government*, in *Collected Writings*, vol. XIX, ed. J. M. Robson (Toronto: University of Toronto Press; London: Routledge & Keagan Paul, 1977), ch. XV. On Mill's "dialectical deliberation," see Dennis F. Thompson, *John Stuart Mill and Representative Government* (Princeton, N.J.: Princeton University Press, 1976), pp. 80–82.

9. Dennis F. Thompson, *The Democratic Citizen: Social Science and Democratic Theory in the Twentieth Century* (Cambridge: Cambridge University Press, 1970), p. 86.

10. Jürgen Habermas, *Between Facts and Norms: Contributions to a Discourse Theory of Law and Democracy* (Cambridge, Mass.: MIT Press, 1996). Also see his "Discourse Ethics," in *Moral Consciousness and Communicative Action*, trans. Christian Lenhardt and Shierry Weber Nicholsen (Cambridge, Mass.: MIT Press, 1993), p. 94.

11. Jefferson to Samuel Kercheval, 12 July 1816, in *The Writings of Thomas Jefferson*, vol. 15, p. 42. For an analysis of Jefferson's attitudes toward constitutional change, see John R. Vile, *The Constitutional Amending Process in American Thought* (New York: Praeger, 1992), pp. 59–78.

12. Although most substantive theories are first-order theories, and many procedural theories are second-order theories, the substantive/procedural distinction is not the same as the first-order/second-order distinction. (See below, chapter 4, note 1.)

13. Joshua Cohen, Review of Robert Dahl's *Democracy and Its Critics*, in *Journal of Politics* 53 (February 1991), pp. 221–25; and "Procedure and Substance in Deliberative Democracy," in S. Benhabib, ed., *Democracy and Difference* (Princeton, N.J.: Princeton University Press, 1996), pp. 95–119; and Jack Knight and James Johnson, "Aggregation and Deliberation: On the Possibility of Democratic Legitimacy," *Political Theory* 22 (May 1994), pp. 277–96. In other writings we have emphasized the contrast between procedural and constitutional conceptions of democracy (see Amy Gutmann

and Dennis Thompson, *Democracy and Disagreement* (Cambridge, Mass.: Harvard University Press, 1996), pp. 27–39), which is the more general distinction applicable to all theories of democracy. It is useful to distinguish our version from others because some deliberative democrats, such as Habermas, are proceduralists, and some liberals who are inclined toward deliberative democracy are constitutionalists. But for the purpose of contrasting deliberative democracy with other conceptions, the distinction between deliberative and aggregative approaches is more relevant.

14. This disagreement is essentially the same as Rawls's "fact of reasonable pluralism." See John Rawls, *Political Liberalism* (New York: Columbia University Press, 1993), pp. 36, 37, 63, 136, 141, 144, 152f, 216f; and Joshua Cohen, "Moral Pluralism and Political Consensus," in David Copp et al., eds., *The Idea of Democracy* (Cambridge: Cambridge University Press, 1993), pp. 270–91.

15. See our discussion of the sources of moral disagreement in Gutmann and Thompson, *Democracy and Disagreement*, pp. 18–26.

16. For a contemporary defense of majoritarianism, see Jeremy Waldron, *The Dignity of Legislation* (Cambridge: Cambridge University Press, 1999), pp. 147–50. On the limits of majority rule, see Gutmann and Thompson, *Democracy and Disagreement*, pp. 27–33.

17. Joseph Schumpeter [*Capitalism, Socialism and Democracy*, 3d ed. (New York: Harper and Row, 1950), p. 269] is the seminal source in the contemporary literature. Anthony Downs gave the theory a more formal and systematic statement, and many political scientists have adopted it with major modifications, but still with enthusiasm. See his *An Economic Theory of Democracy* (New York: Harper and Row, 1957). For a review of the literature, see Bernard Grofman, "Toward an Institution-Rich Theory of Political Competition," in Bernard Grofman, ed., *Information, Participation, and Choice* (Ann Arbor: University of Michigan Press, 1993), p. 193.

18. At least they do so if they can avoid the paradoxes and other technical problems identified by social-choice theorists. For a survey of those problems and an argument showing how deliberative democrats can avoid the problems, see David Miller, "Deliberative Democracy and Social Choice," in David Estlund, ed., *Democracy* (Oxford: Blackwell, 2002), pp. 289–307.

19. See Gutmann and Thompson, *Democracy and Disagreement*, pp. 173–78.

20. E.g., David Estlund, "Beyond Fairness and Deliberation: The Epistemic Dimension of Democratic Authority," in J. Bohman and W. Rehg, eds., *Deliberative Democracy* (Cambridge, Mass.: MIT Press, 1997), pp. 173–204.

21. The expressivist approach is most often proposed as a way of

understanding the act of voting, but it can be applied to political participation and the laws in general, and therefore to the deliberative process. For some general discussions, see Elizabeth S. Anderson, *Value in Ethics and Economics* (Cambridge, Mass.: Harvard University Press, 1993); Elizabeth S. Anderson and Richard H. Pildes, "Expressive Theories of Law: A General Restatement," *University of Pennsylvania Law Review* 148 (May 2000), pp. 1503–75; Cass Sunstein, "Law, Economics and Norms: On the Expressive Function of Law," *University of Pennsylvania Law Review* 144 (May 1996), esp. pp. 2045–49; Robert Nozick, *The Nature of Rationality* (Princeton, N.J.: Princeton University Press, 1993), pp. 26–35; and Nozick, *Philosophical Explanations* (Cambridge, Mass.: Harvard University Press, 1981), pp. 370–80. For criticisms of the approach, see Jeremy Waldron, *Law and Disagreement* (Oxford: Oxford University Press, 1999), pp. 239–41; and Charles R. Beitz, *Political Equality: An Essay in Democratic Theory* (Princeton, N.J.: Princeton University Press, 1989), pp. 93–95.

22. As Jürgen Habermas writes: "all contents, no matter how fundamental the action norm involved may be, must be made to depend on real discourses (or advocatory discourses conducted as substitutes for them)" ["Discourse Ethics," in *Moral Consciousness and Communicative Action*, trans. Christian Lenhardt and Shierry Weber Nicholsen (Cambridge, Mass.: MIT Press, 1993), p. 94]. For comments and other citations, see our discussion in Gutmann and Thompson, *Democracy and Disagreement*, pp. 17–18. Other theorists who would also be more inclined to limit deliberative democracy to process considerations, and are therefore critical of including substantive principles in its theory, include: Jack Knight, "Constitutionalism and Deliberative Democracy," in Stephen Macedo, ed., *Deliberative Politics* (Oxford: Oxford University Press, 1999), pp. 159–69; Cass Sunstein, "Agreement without Theory," in Macedo, pp. 147–48; and Iris Marion Young, "Justice, Inclusion, and Deliberative Democracy," in Macedo, pp. 151–58. For our reply, see Gutmann and Thompson, "Democratic Disagreement," in Macedo, pp. 261–68.

23. See chapter 3, below.

24. Habermas, "Discourse Ethics," p. 261.

25. This can be seen most clearly in his discussion of neutrality: *Political Liberalism* (New York: Columbia University Press, 1993), pp. 190–95, esp. n24.

26. E.g., Michael Sandel, *Democracy's Discontent* (Cambridge Mass.: Harvard University Press, 1996).

27. Gutmann and Thompson, *Democracy and Disagreement*, pp. 18–26.

28. Deliberative disagreements are those in which citizens continue to differ about basic moral principles even though they seek a resolution that is mutually justifiable. The dispute over abortion is an example of a delibera-

tive disagreement, because both sides can justify their views within a reciprocal perspective. A dispute about racial segregation is an example of a nondeliberative disagreement, because one side can be reasonably rejected within a reciprocal perspective. See Gutmann and Thompson, *Democracy and Disagreement*, pp. 2–3, 73–79.

29. For the various arguments on the issue, see Jason A. Beyer, "Public Dilemmas and Gay Marriage" *Journal of Social Philosophy* 33 (Spring 2002), no. 1, pp. 9–16.

30. For one of the most nuanced theories emphasizing popular participation, see Dryzek, *Deliberative Democracy and Beyond*, pp. 81–114. Although Dryzek is primarily concerned to extend deliberative democracy to civil society, and although he does not deny the importance of representation, the institutions about which he is evidently most enthusiastic are robustly participatory. See also the participatory approach presented in the editors' introduction, and in most articles, in Archon Fung and Olin Wright, eds., *Deepening Democracy* (London and New York: Verso, 2003).

31. See Joshua Cohen, "Deliberation and Democratic Legitimacy," in Estlund, ed., *Democracy*, pp. 101, and 106, n. 28; and Thomas E. Cronin, *Direct Democracy: The Politics of Initiative, Referendum and Recall* (Cambridge, Mass.: Harvard University Press, 1999), pp. 38–59.

32. James S. Fishkin, *The Voice of the People: Public Opinion and Democracy* (New Haven: Yale University Press, 1995).

33. Jürgen Habermas, "Deliberative Politics" in Estlund, ed., *Democracy*, pp. 114–15, 120–21.

34. Joshua Cohen, "Deliberation and Democratic Legitimacy," in Estlund, ed., *Democracy*, pp. 101–3; and Jane Mansbridge, "Everyday Talk in the Deliberative System," in Macedo, ed., *Deliberative Politics*, pp. 211–39.

35. Cohen, "Deliberation and Democratic Legitimacy," p. 102.

36. "Investors are seeking a new gold standard for corporate governance, and they are putting a lot of companies onto their post-Enron punch list," according to Patrick S. McGurn, senior vice president of Institutional Shareholder Services [quoted in Claudia H. Deutsch, "The Revolt of the Shareholders," *New York Times*, February 23, 2003, sec. 3, p. 1].

37. Amy Gutmann, *Democratic Education* (Princeton, N.J.: Princeton University Press, 1999), pp. 50–52, 292–303, and *passim*.

38. For a skeptical view of the internet's potential to promote genuine deliberation, see Cass Sunstein, *Democracy.com* (Princeton, N.J.: Princeton University Press, 2002). A more optimistic view of the internet's potential with regard to deliberation can be found at http://www.stanford.edu/group/siqss/itandsociety/v01i01/v01i01a20.pdf [accessed 27 October 03].

39. "20 Most Popular Search Terms at 10 Leading Portals and

Search Engines March 1999 to January 2001" (two-year study by Alexa Research), cited in Michael Pastore, "Search Engines, Browsers Still Confusing Many Web Users" at http://cyberatlas.internet.com/big_picture/traffic_patterns/article/0,,5931_588851,00.html [accessed 11 March 03].

40. Exceptions are John S. Dryzek, "Transnational Democracy," *Journal of Political Philosophy* 7 (1999), pp. 30–51; and Dennis F. Thompson, "Democratic Theory and Global Society," *Journal of Political Philosophy* 7 (1999), pp. 111–25.

41. Joseph Raz, "Disagreement in Politics," *American Journal of Jurisprudence* 43 (1998), pp. 25–52.

42. Stanley Fish, "Mutual Respect as a Device of Exclusion," in Macedo, ed., *Deliberative Politics*, pp. 88–102. A more nuanced version of the power-oriented objection is Ian Shapiro, "Enough of Deliberation," also in Macedo, pp. 28–38; and *The State of Democratic Theory* (New Haven: Yale University Press, 2003), pp. 22–26.

43. The argument for such a commission is similar to the case for establishing independent bodies to carry out electoral redistricting, which in the United States suffers from some of the same problems. See Dennis F. Thompson, *Just Elections* (Chicago: Chicago University Press, 2002), pp. 173–79.

44. Lynn Sanders, "Against Deliberation," *Political Theory* 25:3 (1997), pp. 347–76.

45. See http://bioethics.gov/reports/cloningreport/index.html [accessed 11 March 03].

46. Cass Sunstein, "The Law of Group Polarization," *Journal of Political Philosophy* 10 (2), p. 176. Cass Sunstein, *Why Societies Need More Dissent* (Cambridge, Mass.: Harvard University Press, 2003), chapter 6.

47. James Fishkin and R. Luskin, "Bringing Deliberation to the Democratic Dialogue: the NIC and Beyond," in *A Poll with a Human Face: the National Issues Convention Experiment in Political Communication*, ed. M. McCombs and A. Reynolds (New York: Erlbaum, 1999), pp. 30–38.

48. Michael Walzer, "Deliberation, and What Else?" in Macedo, ed., p. 67.

49. We discuss this case at length in *Democracy and Disagreement*, but use it there for a somewhat different purpose: to explain the limits on the kinds of reasons that are appropriate in deliberation (pp. 63–69).

50. *Mozert v. Hawkins County Bd. of Educ.*, 827 F. 2d 1058 (6th Cir. 1987), *cert. denied*, 484 U.S. 1066 (1988) at 1065.

51. William Galston, "Diversity, Toleration, and Deliberative Democracy," in Macedo, ed., pp. 39–48.

52. Galston, pp. 43–44.

53. Thompson, *Just Elections*, esp. pp. 138–39.

54. David Held, *Democracy and the Global Order: From the Modern State to Cosmopolitan Governance* (Stanford, Calif.: Stanford University Press, 1995), p. 237.

Chapter 2
Moral Conflict and Political Consensus

We received helpful comments on drafts of this article from many people, and especially wish to thank Jane Mansbridge, Henry Richardson, Alan Wertheimer, Ken Winston, the *Ethics* reviewers, and an associate editor of *Ethics*. A slightly different version of this article appears in R. Bruce Douglass, Gerald Mara, and Henry Richardson, eds., *Liberalism and the Good* (New York: Routledge, Chapman & Hall, 1990).

1. For example, John Rawls, "Justice as Fairness: Political not Metaphysical," *Philosophy and Public Affairs* 14 (1985), pp. 248–51; Thomas Nagel, "Moral Conflict and Political Legitimacy," *Philosophy and Public Affairs* 16 (1987), pp. 223–27; and David A. J. Richards, *Toleration and the Constitution* (New York: Oxford University Press, 1986), pp. 67–162.

2. For a more thorough discussion of several relevant meanings of neutrality and their application to a procedural theory, see John Rawls, "The Priority of the Right and Ideas of the Good," *Philosophy and Public Affairs* 17 (1988), pp. 260–64. For a defense of neutrality in the justification of governmental policies, directed against communitarianism and perfectionism, see Will Kymlicka, "Liberal Individualism and Liberal Neutrality," *Ethics* 99 (1989), pp. 883–905.

3. The argument we present is in its essentials found in Locke's *A Letter Concerning Toleration*, ed. James Tully (Indianapolis: Hackett, 1983), pp. 23–39. We call the argument Lockean, however, to indicate that we do not claim that every element of our reconstruction, especially our applications to contemporary problems, is precisely faithful to Locke's intention or even his text. Also, we ignore a number of arguments that were important for Locke and his contemporaries—e.g., the argument against tolerating atheists and Catholics. The claims that people who do not believe in God cannot be trusted to keep promises, and that people who owe allegiance to the pope cannot be trusted to obey a secular authority, are distinct from those that underlie Locke's general defense of toleration.

4. Ibid., pp. 23–25.

5. Nagel, "Moral Conflict and Political Legitimacy," p. 229.

6. Ibid., p. 235.

7. Locke, *A letter Concerning Toleration*, pp. 27–28.

8. Ibid., pp. 23, 26–29, and 38.

9. A helpful short analysis, which goes beyond the formal criteria that are usually advanced to identify a moral position, is Ronald Dworkin's "The Concept of a Moral Position," in his "Lord Devlin and the Enforcement of Morals," in Richard Wasserstrom, ed., *Morality and the Law* (Belmont, Calif.: Wadsworth, 1971), pp. 61–67.

10. Many substantive positions satisfy this requirement. For example, an "ethics of care," a morality that admits greater obligations to closely related people than to distantly related people or to humanity more generally, can be adopted by all members of a society, regardless of their class, race, or sex. The commonly drawn contrast between an "ethics of principle" and an "ethics of care" is not between a moral point of view and an amoral one. But some commonly encountered arguments do not satisfy the requirement of a moral point of view—e.g., an argument to restrict the basic liberties of a minority simply on the grounds that members of the majority have a preference for restricting their liberty. Such a position could not reasonably be adopted by a member of the minority and therefore fails to qualify as a moral point of view.

11. For a helpful discussion of the foundations of the deliberative ideal, see Joshua Cohen, "Deliberation and Democratic Legitimacy," in Alan Hamlin and Philip Pettit, eds., *The Good Polity: Normative Analysis of the State* (Oxford: Blackwell, 1989), pp. 17–34. Also see Charles Larmore, *Patterns of Moral Complexity* (Cambridge: Cambridge University Press, 1987), esp. pp. 59–66; and Bernard Manin, "On Legitimacy and Political Deliberation," *Political Theory* 15 (1987), pp. 338–68.

12. Roger Wertheimer, "Understanding the Abortion Argument," in Marshall Cohen et al., eds., *The Rights and Wrongs of Abortion* (Princeton, N.J.: Princeton University Press, 1974), pp. 23–51.

13. Ibid., pp. 31, 37.

14. Ibid., p. 41.

15. Ibid., pp. 50–51.

16. In contrast to what has been called recognition respect (what we owe all persons simply by virtue of their being persons), mutual respect is a form of appraisal respect; it expresses a positive appraisal of a person for manifesting some excellence of character. This "enables us to see that there is no puzzle at all in thinking both that all persons are entitled to respect just by virtue of their being persons and that persons are deserving of more or less respect by virtue of their personal characteristics" (Stephen L. Darwall, "Two Kinds of Respect," *Ethics* 88 [1977], p. 46, also 38–39, 45).

17. On the significance of some of these qualities for democratic character, see Albert Hirschman, "Having Opinions—One of the Elements

of Well-Being?" *American Economic Association Papers and Proceedings* 79 (1989), pp. 75–79.

18. Quoted in Joseph A. Califano, Jr., *Governing America* (New York: Simon & Schuster, 1981), p. 84.

19. Remarks of Congressman Bill Green (R-N.Y.), *Congressional Record*, September 9, 1988, p. H7351.

20. However, Congressman Green's opponents did not draw the conclusion that he wished them to draw from the existence of moral controversy: that "the decision as to what should happen to the product of that rape . . . is best left to the woman's own conscience" (ibid.). In effect, he was invoking a version of the neutrality argument to try to remove the issue from the political agenda.

21. Remarks of William Dannemeyer (R-Calif.), *Congressional Record*, September 22, 1983, p. H7319. Although Dannemeyer also said that the "economic consequences of the moral issue should not be permitted to resolve the matter," his entire speech was devoted to the "fiscal consequences."

22. Representative Barbara Mikulski (D-Md.), *Congressional Record*, September 22, 1983, p. H7319.

23. For insights into the significance of openness for democratic character, see Hirschman, "Having Opinions."

24. Califano, p. 68 (emphasis added). Califano also comments that he should do all he could to avoid "unnecessary provocation."

25. "Religious Belief and Public Morality: A Catholic Governor's Perspective," September 13, 1984, pp. 17–18, photocopy. We are grateful to Ken Winston for calling our attention to this passage.

26. The requirement of an economy of moral disagreement appears to resemble Larmore's "universal norm of rational dialogue," which he explains (see note 11) as follows: "When two people disagree about some specific point, but wish to continue talking about the more general problem they wish to solve, each should prescind from the beliefs that the other rejects, (1) in order to construct an argument on the basis of his other beliefs that will convince the other of the truth of the disputed belief, or (2) in order to shift to another aspect of the problem, where the possibilities of agreement seem greater" (p. 53). There are, however, important differences between Larmore's understanding and ours. On our understanding of mutual respect, people who disagree (but wish to continue talking) need not prescind from publicly professing beliefs that others reject. Nor should they "retreat to neutral grounds." Instead, they should search for common ground (and their search should satisfy the standards of mutual respect). An economy of moral disagreement aspires to a mutual commitment to substantive moral principles that are not necessarily neutral either

with respect to prevailing conceptions of the good life or even to the specific controversy. It should also be clear from the place of an economy of moral disagreement within a broader public philosophy that the recommendation to prescind from invoking values at odds with some citizens' beliefs is contingent upon those beliefs' meeting the threshold requirements of a respectable moral position.

27. The search for an economy of moral disagreement should not be identified with Rawls's search for an overlapping consensus. In our view, an economy of moral disagreement is not a defining feature of a political theory. It is only one form that respectful accommodation of moral conflict may take in a pluralist society in those cases in which conflicting moral perspectives fortuitously converge in their practical implications. Compare n. 36 below.

28. Judith Jarvis Thomson, "A Defense of Abortion," in Cohen et al., eds., pp. 3–22.

29. Ibid., pp. 4–5.

30. Roe v. Wade, 410 U.S. 113 (1973), pp. 162–64.

31. Ibid., pp. 163–64.

32. William L. Webster et al. v. Reproductive Health Services et al., 57 LW 5023–5045 (June 27, 1989). See esp. Justice O'Connor's concurring opinion at 5033–34, and compare Blackmun's partial dissent at 5037.

33. See Akron v. Akron Center for Reproductive Health, Inc., 462 U.S. 416 (1983).

34. For some examples of characteristics of legislative institutions, especially the Congress, that encourage and discourage deliberation, see Jane Mansbridge, "Motivating Deliberation in Congress," in Sarah Baumgartner Thurow, ed., *Constitutionalism in America* (New York: University Press of America, 1988), vol. 2, pp. 59–86.

35. See, for example, Alasdair MacIntyre, *After Virtue* (Notre Dame, Ind.: University of Notre Dame Press, 1981), esp. pp. 6, 20–21, 189; and Michael Sandel, *Liberalism and the Limits of Justice* (New York: Cambridge University Press, 1982), esp. p. 183.

36. John Rawls, "The Idea of an Overlapping Consensus," *Oxford Journal of Legal Studies* 7 (1987), pp. 1–25.

37. Ibid., pp. 17, 20–21.

38. Rawls recognizes that some questions properly included on the political agenda will be controversial because they are so important that differences over them "have to be fought out, even should this mean civil war," or presumably because they are as yet unresolvable by a political conception of justice. In both cases, however, the aim of a political conception of justice, on Rawls's account, is to create an overlapping consensus and thereby decrease political controversy (ibid., p. 13).

39. Ibid., p. 14.

Chapter 3
Deliberative Democracy beyond Process

1. As Jürgen Habermas writes, "All contents, no matter how fundamental the action norm involved may be, must be made to depend on real discourses (or advisory discourses conducted as substitutes for them)." "Discourse ethics," in *Moral Consciousness and Communicative Action*, trans. Christian Lenhardt and Shierry Weber Nicholsen (Cambridge, Mass.: MIT Press, 1993), p. 94. For comments and other citations, see our discussion in Amy Gutmann and Dennis Thompson, *Democracy and Disagreement* (Cambridge, Mass.: Harvard University Press, 1996), pp. 17–18. Other theorists, who would also be more inclined to limit deliberative democracy to process considerations and are therefore critical of including substantive principles in its theory, include: Jack Knight, "Constitutionalism and Deliberative Democracy," in Stephen Macedo, ed., *Deliberative Politics* (New York: Oxford University Press, 1999), pp. 159–69; Cass Sunstein, "Agreement Without Theory," in Macedo, pp. 147–48; and Iris Marion Young, "Justice, Inclusion, and Deliberative Democracy," in Macedo, pp. 151–58. For our reply, see Gutmann and Thompson, "Democratic disagreement," in Macedo, pp. 261–68.

2. See statements by NICE's newly appointed director, Michael Rawlins, in Richard Horton, "NICE: A Step Forward in the Quality of NHS Care," *The Lancet* 353 (March 27, 1999), pp. 1028–29; and Gavin Yamey, "Chairman of NICE Admits That Its Judgments Are Hard to Defend," *British Medical Journal* 319 (November 6, 1999), p. 1222.

3. See "NICE appraisal of Zanamivir (Relenza)" posted at www.nice.org.uk. For some of the reaction, see Stephen D. Moore, "U.K. Rebuffs Glaxo on New Flu Drug," *Wall Street Journal* (October 11, 1999), p. A19.

4. Stuart Hampshire, *Innocence and Experience* (Cambridge, Mass.: Harvard University Press, 1989), p. 112.

5. Ibid, p. 112.

6. See "NICE Appraisal of Zanamivir (Relenza)." For some of the reaction, see Moore, "U.K. Rebuffs Glaxo on New Flu Drug." The Food and Drug Administration approved Relenza for use in the United States despite a 13–4 vote of an outside panel of experts recommending against approval. Some critics believe that the drug was overprescribed during a recent flu season. See Sheryl Gay Stolberg, "F.D.A. Warns of Overuse of two New Drugs Against Flu," *New York Times* (January 13, 2000), p. A18.

7. See House of Commons debate, November 10, 1999, and discussion above, pp. 119–20.

8. House of Commons debate, November 10, 1999. Also see Jo Lenaghan, "The Rationing Debate: Central Government Should Have a Greater Role in Rationing Decisions," *British Medical Journal* 314 (March 29, 1997), 967–71.

9. Gutmann and Thompson, *Democracy and Disagreement*, pp. 199–229.

10. Not so welcome are other critics—those who reject the aim of giving substantive content to the claims of reciprocity, or who reject the very standard of reciprocity. But neither are their claims cogent. Having rejected the idea of mutual justification, they are hard-pressed to explain how they can justify (at all) imposing coercive laws and policies on citizens who morally disagree with them. See the section "A Public Philosophy" in chapter 2, and Gutmann and Thompson, *Democracy and Disagreement*, pp. 352–53.

11. The discussion here of moral and political provisionality draws on our analysis in "Why Deliberative Democracy is Different," in Ellen Frankel Paul et al., eds., *Democracy* (Cambridge: Cambridge University Press, 2000), pp. 161–80 [chapter 4 of the present volume].

12. The range is determined by what we call "deliberative disagreements," which are those in which citizens continue to differ about basic moral principles even though they seek a resolution that is mutually justifiable. The dispute over abortion is an example of a deliberative disagreement, because both sides can justify their views within a reciprocal perspective. A dispute about racial segregation is an example of a nondeliberative disagreement, because one side can be reasonably rejected within a reciprocal perspective. See Gutmann and Thompson, *Democracy and Disagreement*, pp. 2–3, 73–79.

13. E. Rous et al., "A Purchase Experience of Managing New Expensive Drugs: Interferon Beta," *British Medical Journal* 313 (November 9, 1996), pp. 1195–96.

14. Gutmann and Thompson, *Democracy and Disagreement*, pp. 57–58.

15. Ibid., p. 353.

16. Frederick Schauer, "Talking as a Decision Procedure," in Macedo, pp. 17–27.

Chapter 4
Why Deliberative Democracy Is Different

1. Although most substantive theories are first-order theories, and many procedural theories are second-order theories, the substantive/procedural distinction is not the same as the first-order/second-order distinction. The substantive/procedural distinction characterizes theories according to whether they justify political decisions by reference to independent moral

principles or entirely by reference to features of the process. The first-order/second-order distinction classifies theories according to whether they affirm the truth of a single consistent set of (substantive or procedural) principles that exclude other such principles, or whether they refer to the principles in a way that is consistent with a range of potentially inconsistent sets (for example, by prescribing certain attitudes or conduct with regard to the principles and the persons who hold them).

2. See Amy Gutmann and Dennis Thompson, *Democracy and Disagreement* (Cambridge, Mass.: Harvard University Press, 1996).

Chapter 5
Just Deliberation about Health Care

1. Karen Grandstrand Gervais et al., eds., *Ethical Challenges in Managed Care* (Washington, D.C.: Georgetown University Press, 1999), chaps. 1, 19, and 20. The rescreening test PAPNET seems to be the model for PUREPAP in the case study. *Medical Industry Today* (August 3, 1998) and *Biomedical Market Newsletter* (February 28, 1998) report on this test. *Biomedical Market Newsletter* reports that PAPNET would cost $33,781 for each abnormal Pap smear identified and $101,343 for each HPV identified, compared to $1,065 and $4,970, respectively, for manual rescreening. It also reports the results of a new CDC study released January 31, 1998 (Pt. 2): "Given the high costs of using the automated system, the study suggests other ways to reduce cervical cancer death. These include implementing more effective screening programs, such as performing Pap smears on women who do not currently receive them. . . ."

2. Amy Gutmann and Dennis Thompson, *Democracy and Disagreement* (Cambridge, Mass.: Harvard University Press, 1996).

3. Lawrence C. Becker, *Reciprocity* (London: Routledge and Kegan Paul, 1986), pp. 73–144.

4. Gutmann and Thompson, 1996, pp. 208–29.

5. Gutmann and Thompson, "Deliberating about Bioethics," *Hastings Center Report* (May/June 1997), pp. 38–41.

6. Gervais et al., pp. 17–18.

7. Kurt Baier, *The Moral Point of View* (Ithaca, N.Y.: Cornell University Press, 1958), pp. 187–213; John Rawls, *A Theory of Justice* (Cambridge, Mass.: Harvard University Press, 1971), pp. 130–136.

8. Gervais et al., p. 18.

9. Gervais et al., p. 24.

10. John Stuart Mill, *Considerations on Representative Government* (London: Longman, Green, and Roberts, 1865), chap. III, p. 68.

11. Gutmann and Thompson, 1996, pp. 2–3, 73–79.

Chapter 6
The Moral Foundations of Truth Commissions

1. "South Africa Looks for Truth and Hopes for Reconciliation," *The Economist* (20 April 1996), p. 33.

2. We discuss only some of the most important and most general justifications here. In practice the TRC emphasized different purposes at different stages of its process. (See Andre du Toit, "The Moral Foundations of the South African TRC," in Robert I. Rotberg and Dennis Thompson, eds., *Truth v. Justice: The Morality of Truth Commissions* [Princeton, N.J.: Princeton University Press], pp. 122–40.) One of the most extensive defenses of the TRC lists fourteen different goals. But virtually all are particular forms of a limited number of the more general justifications, and in fact the authors themselves examine only a few in any detail. See Kadar Asmal, Louise Asmal, and Ronald Suresh Roberts, *Reconciliation through Truth* (New York: Palgrave Macmillan, 1998), pp. 10–11. The commission itself presented its primary objective as promoting "national unity and reconciliation," but interpreted it to include various other purposes, such as "promotion of democracy," restoring the "dignity of victims," and encouraging "perpetrators . . . to come to terms with their own past." Truth and Reconciliation Commission, *Final Report* (Cape Town, 29 October 1998), I, ch. 4, "The Mandate," sections 2, 3, and 31.

3. Asmal et al., *Reconciliation*, pp. 12–27 (emphasis added). This argument often takes the form of appealing to a different kind of justice, usually called "restorative." See Archbishop Desmond Tutu's comments in the Foreword, TRC, *Final Report*, I, chap. 1, section 36; the TRC's discussion of "concepts and principles" in I, chap. 5, sections 80–100; and Elizabeth Kiss, "Moral Ambition Within and Beyond Political Constraints," and Andre du Toit, "The Moral Foundations of the South African TRC," both in *Truth v. Justice*. See also the section of this chapter entitled "The Compassionate Response."

4. Tutu seems to suggest that "shaming" may serve as a partial substitute for criminal punishment (*Final Report*, I, chap. 1, section 36).

5. Tina Rosenberg, "Recovering from Apartheid," *New Yorker* (18 November 1996), p. 92.

6. Asmal et al., *Reconciliation*, pp. 19, 22.

7. Mark Gevisser, "The Witnesses," *New York Times Magazine* (22 June 1997), p. 32.

8. The TRC explicitly acknowledged that in carrying out its function of identifying perpetrators of gross human rights abuses, it gave greater weight to its "truth-seeking role . . . the public interest in the exposure of wrongdoing" than to the "fair treatment of individuals in what was not a

court of law." It used a lower burden of proof than that required by the criminal justice system (*Final Report*, I, chap. 4, pp. 153–55). However, the amnesty hearings followed more closely the adversarial and judicial procedures. On some limitations of any appeal to due process, see Sanford Levinson, "Trials, Commissions, and Investigative Committees," in *Truth v. Justice*, pp. 211—34.

9. For a statement of this aspect of the "realist" position, see Dumisa Ntsebexa, "The Uses of Truth Commissions," in *Truth v. Justice*, pp. 158–79.

10. *Final Report*, I, chap. 1, section 11.

11. Rosenberg, p. 51.

12. See Rajeev Bhargava, "Restoring Decency to Barbaric Societies," in *Truth v. Justice*, pp. 45–62.

13. For the strengths and weaknesses of the therapeutic approach, see Martha Minow, "The Hope for Healing," in *Truth v. Justice*, pp. 235–60.

14. Asmal et al., *Reconciliation*, p. 49.

15. See citations in note 3 above.

16. Suzanne Daley, "In Apartheid Inquiry, Agony Is Relived but Not Put to Rest," *New York Times* (17 July 1997), p. A10.

17. Timothy Garten Ash, "True Confessions," *New York Review of Books* (17 July 1997), pp. 36–37.

18. Rosenberg, "Recovering," p. 95. (See also citations in note 3, above.)

19. Some forward-looking, political, and inclusive goals for the South African Commission are articulated by Alex Boraine, "Truth and Reconciliation in South Africa," in *Truth v. Justice*, pp. 141–57.

20. The phrase is from a statement made by Tutu during the hearings, quoted in Ash, "True Confessions," p. 37. For a different perspective, see Boraine, "Truth and Reconciliation."

21. Ash, "True Confessions," 37.

22. See Asmal et al., *Reconciliation*, p. 46; and Mark Osiel, *Mass Atrocity, Collective Memory and the Law* (New Brunswick, N.J.: Transaction, 1999), pp. 210–11.

23. Asmal et al., *Reconciliation*, p. 47.

24. Ibid, p. 47.

25. Michel Foucault, "Film and Popular Memory," *Radical Philosophy* XI (1975), pp. 24, 25.

26. For a discussion of the difficulties in deliberately creating collective memory, see Osiel, *Mass Atrocity*, pp. 209–12.

27. See *Final Report*, IV, sections 60–81.

28. The National Unity and Reconciliation Act that created the TRC set this goal: "Establishing as complete a picture as possible of the

causes, nature and extent of the gross violations of human rights which were committed during the period from March 1960 to the cut-off date, including the antecedents, circumstances, factors and context of such violations, as well as the perspectives of the victims and the motives and perspectives of the persons responsible for the commission of the violations . . ." (*Final Report*, I, chap. 4, section 31). In the end, the commission did not claim that it had succeeded in presenting a "complete picture," and in its "perpetrator findings" (V, chap. 6, sections 77–150) it followed a more cautious, judicial approach. But many of the general conclusions of the report have the character of an authoritative historical verdict (see, for example, I, chap. 2; II, chaps. 1, 3–5).

29. *Final Report*, V, chap. 6, sections 52–62, "The Commission's Shortcomings." At the conference at which an earlier version of this chapter was presented to members of the commission and staff, the authors suggested that the final report might include a candid discussion of its own limitations.

30. Asmal et al., *Reconciliation*, 46. For a description of "contrapuntal history," which is consistent with this approach, see Charles Maier, "Doing History, Doing Justice," in *Truth v. Justice*, pp. 261–78.

31. This conception of democracy, including the value of reciprocity and the idea of an economy of moral disagreement that we present here, is developed more systematically in Amy Gutmann and Dennis Thompson, *Democracy and Disagreement* (Cambridge, Mass.: Harvard University Press, 1996).

32. Lawrence C. Becker, *Reciprocity* (London: Routledge and Kegan Paul, 1986), pp. 73–144.

33. Although the commission apparently adopted a notion of restorative justice, it went to some length to try to justify giving priority to this value over ordinary criminal justice. See the *Final Report*, I, chap. 5, sections 53–100.

34. For a valuable discussion of the commission's hearings on the role of judges and lawyers, see David Dyzenhaus, *Judging the Judges, Judging Ourselves: Truth, Reconciliation and the Apartheid Legal Order* (Oxford: Oxford University Press, 1998). Also, see the discussion of the institutional hearings, especially on business and labor, the legal community, the health sector, and the media, in the *Final Report*, IV, chaps. 2, 4–6.

35. For a complementary perspective on the value of deliberation by truth commissions, see David Crocker, "Truth Commissions, Transitional Justice and Civil Society," in *Truth v. Justice*, pp. 99–121.

36. See Gutmann and Thompson, *Democracy and Disagreement*, pp. 85–94.

37. Rosenberg, "Recovering," p. 90.

38. Ibid., pp. 89–90.

39. Hannah Arendt, *The Human Condition* (New York: Doubleday, 1959), pp. 217–218.

40. Second Submission of the National Party to the Truth and Reconciliation Commission, May 1997, "General Comments," p. 8 (available on the official TRC website [www.truth.org.za] under Human Rights Violations Committee, Submissions, National Party).

Acknowledgments

Chapter 2. "Moral Conflict and Political Consensus," *Ethics* (October 1990), vol. 100, pp. 64–88. Reprinted in R. Bruce Douglass et al., eds., *Liberalism and the Good* (London: Routledge, Chapman and Hall, 1990).

Chapter 3. "Deliberative Democracy Beyond Process," *Journal of Political Philosophy* (June 2002), vol. 10, pp. 153–74. Reprinted in P. Laslett and J. Fishkin, eds., *Debating Deliberative Democracy*, vol. 7 in the series *Philosophy, Politics and Society* (Oxford: Blackwell, 2003), pp. 31–53.

Chapter 4. "Why Deliberative Democracy Is Different," *Social Philosophy and Policy* (Winter 2000), vol. 17, pp. 161–80. Reprinted in Ellen Frankel Paul et al., eds., *Democracy* (Cambridge: Cambridge, University Press, 2000). Translated and reprinted in *Philosophique* (Autumn 2002), vol. 29, pp. 193–214.

Chapter 5. "Just Deliberation about Health Care," in M. Danis, C. Clancy, and L. Churchill, eds., *Ethical Dimensions of Health Policy* (Oxford: Oxford University Press, 2002), pp. 77–94.

Chapter 6. "The Moral Foundations of Truth Commissions," in Robert I. Rotberg and Dennis Thompson, eds., *Truth v. Justice. The Morality of Truth Commissions* (Princeton, N.J.: Princeton University Press, 2000), pp. 22–44.

Previous Works Jointly Authored by
Amy Gutmann & Dennis Thompson

"Democratic decisions about health care: Why be like NICE?" in Bill New and Julia Neuberger, eds., *Hidden Assets: Value and Decision-Making in the NHS* (London: King's Fund Publishing, 2002), pp. 111–28.

"Deliberative Democracy," in P. B. Clarke and J. Foweraker, eds., *Encyclopedia of Democratic Thought* (London: Routledge, 2001).

"Democratic Disagreement," in Stephen Macedo, ed., *Deliberative Politics: Essays on 'Democracy and Disagreement'* (Oxford: Oxford University Press, 1999), pp. 243–79.

"Disagreeing about Deliberative Democracy," in *The Good Society* (Fall 1997), vol. 7, pp. 11–15.

"Deliberating about Bioethics," in *Hastings Center Report* (May/June 1997), pp. 38–41.

Democracy and Disagreement (Cambridge, Mass.: Harvard University Press, 1996). Excerpts reprinted in Andreas Hess, ed., *American Social and Political Thought* (New York: New York University Press, 2003).Translated and reprinted in Stepfano Cochetti, ed., *Filosofia e Questioni Publiche*, vol. 5 (Rome: Luiss Edizioni, 2000).

"Moral Disagreement in a Democracy," in *Social Philosophy and Policy* (Winter 1995), vol. 12, pp. 87–110; also in Ellen Frankel Paul et al., eds., *Contemporary Social and Political Philosophy* (Cambridge: Cambridge University Press, 1996).

"The Theory of Legislative Ethics," in Bruce Jennings and Daniel Callahan, eds., *Representation and Responsibility: Exploring Legislative Ethics* (New York and London: Plenum Press, 1985), pp. 167–95.

Ethics and Politics: Cases and Comments (Chicago, Ill.: Nelson-Hall, 1984; third edition, 1997).

Index

Crocker, David, 204n.35
Cronin, Thomas E., 193n.31
Cunningham, Frank, 190n.3
Cuomo, Mario, 85

Daley, Suzanne, 203n.16
Dannemeyer, William, 197n.21
Darwall, Stephen L., 196n.16
decision-making: in aggregative conceptions
of democracy, 14–15, 17; mutually respectful processes of, 11; openness regarding in deliberative democracy, 18–21
(*see also* moral disagreement); political
sovereignty of citizens in, 96. *See also*
proceduralism
de Klerk, Fredrik Willem, 185–86
de Kock, Eugene, 167, 183
deliberation: bargaining as alternative to,
113–15; biases in, 48–53; burdens of injustice and, 142–44; democratic inclusion
as measure of, 9–10; institutional changes
furthering, 89–90; justification and provisionality, 111–13 (*see also* provisionality);
justification through public, 27, 43–45,
62–63, 98–102, 107, 133–34 (*see also* reciprocity); key components of, 133; limited
generosity and, 10–11; power and, 46–48;
preclusion requirements and, 73; redun-
dancy, claims of, 43–45; reiteration of,
158 (*see also* provisionality); as requirement of deliberative democracy, 4–5; resolution of moral conflict through, 12–13
(*see also* moral disagreement); scope of
(*see* scope of deliberation); teaching of
knowledge and skills, need for, 35–36;
value of, instrumental and noninstrumental, 134
deliberation, examples of: in a for-profit
HMO, 140, 145–50, 154–56; health-care
priorities in the United Kingdom, 57, 97–
98, 101–5, 109, 112–15, 117–20, 123; rationing of Medicaid resources in Oregon,
17–20, 22; stem cell research, 52–53;
truth commissions (*see* truth commissions); war against Iraq, decision to wage,
1–8, 37–38, 40–42, 62–63
deliberative democracy: advantages of, 19–
21, 135–36; aggregative conceptions of
democracy and (*see* aggregative conceptions of democracy); as an aspirational

ideal, 37; characteristics of, 3–7; criticisms of, 18–19, 40–56, 136; definition of,
7; democratic inclusion as test of, 9–10;
disagreements within (*see* disagreements
within deliberative democracy); the future of (*see* future of deliberative democracy, the); health care decisions and (*see*
health care); moral and political judgments, conflict of, 119–24; moral disagreement and (*see* moral disagreement);
origins of, 8–9; practical objections to,
48–56; principles of, 133–135; proceduralism and (*see* proceduralism); provisionality and (*see* provisionality); purposes of,
10–13; reason-giving requirement of, 3–4;
reciprocity in (*see* reciprocity); scope of
(*see* scope of deliberation); as second-
order theory, 13, 127, 132; substantive
principles, need for in, 95–98, 102–10,
118–24, 136–38 (*see also* proceduralism;
provisionality); theoretical objections to,
40–48; truth commissions and, 178–81,
187 (*see also* truth commissions)
deliberative disagreements, 28–29, 151–52,
192–93n.28, 200n.12. *See also* mutual
respect
deliberative polling, 31, 54
Democracy and Disagreement
(Gutmann/Thompson), 46, 95–96, 107,
110, 121, 127, 133, 191nn.13, 15, 16, 19,
192nn.22, 27, 193n.28, 194n.49, 199n.1,
200nn.9, 10, 12, 14, 15, 201nn.2, 4, 11,
204nn. 31, 36
democratic accountability. *See* accountability
democratic theory: aggregative *vs.* deliberative, 13–17; consensual *vs.* pluralist, 26–
29; deliberative democracy (*see* deliberative democracy); first- and second-order
distinguished, 13, 126–27, 200n.1; instrumental *vs.* expressive, 21–23; moral disagreement, responses to, 127–32 (*see also*
moral disagreement); procedural and constitutional conceptions, contrast between,
190–91n.13; representative *vs.* participatory, 30–31, 193n.30; substantive *vs.* procedural (*see* proceduralism)
DesertHealth, 140, 145–50, 154–56
Deutsch, Claudia, 193n.36
Dewey, John, 9